# THE INDUSTRIAL POLICY OF AUSTRALIA

ORGANISATION FOR ECONOMIC CO-OPERATION AND DEVELOPMENT

*The Organisation for Economic Co-operation and Development (OECD) was set up under a Convention signed in Paris on 14th December, 1960, which provides that the OECD shall promote policies designed:*

- *to achieve the highest sustainable economic growth and employment and a rising standard of living in Member countries, while maintaining financial stability, and thus to contribute to the development of the world economy;*
- *to contribute to sound economic expansion in Member as well as non-member countries in the process of economic development;*
- *to contribute to the expansion of world trade on a multilateral, non-discriminatory basis in accordance with international obligations.*

*The Members of OECD are Australia, Austria, Belgium, Canada, Denmark, Finland, France, the Federal Republic of Germany, Greece, Iceland, Ireland, Italy, Japan, Luxembourg, the Netherlands, New Zealand, Norway, Portugal, Spain, Sweden, Switzerland, Turkey, the United Kingdom and the United States.*

***





Director of Information, OECD
2, rue André-Pascal, 75775 PARIS CEDEX 16, France.

## FOREWORD

by

A. Coessens
Director-General for Industry
Ministry of Economic Affairs
(Belgium)
and Chairman of the OECD Industry Committee

This report is based on a summary of the information provided by the Australian authorities on the occasion of the review of this country's industrial policy carried out by the Industry Committee at a plenary meeting held in November 1974. This information was updated as necessary until the beginning of May 1975. The conclusions summarize the main aspects which the Committee found of particular interest and puts forward a few practical considerations which, the Committee believed could be useful to the Australian authorities in formulating and reviewing their industrial policies.

This report is one of a series analysing the industrial policies of Member countries considered either individually or together. * These reports contain information and analyses of the questions facing governments in this area, the aims they are pursuing and the instruments at their disposal, as seen by those responsible for formulating and implementing industrial policies in their respective countries.

The review carried out by the Industry Committee and on which this report was based was prepared by three Delegates to the Committee chosen as rapporteurs and belonging respectively to the German, Japanese and Swedish Delegations, and by Mr. L. F. Drahotsky (Canada), my predecessor as Chairman of the Industry Committee.

On behalf of the Industry Committee, I should like to take this opportunity to thank the Australian authorities, and in particular Ambassador R. J. Cameron, Permanent Representative to OECD, who insisted on personally presenting the review of Australia's industrial policy to the Committee, Mr. A. J. Woods and Mr. F. R. Somes, respectively Deputy Secretary and Assistant Secretary in the Department of Manufacturing Industry, and Mr. G. J. Hall and Mr. D. C. Hawes,

* For particulars on OECD publications in this field, see Bibliography at the end of the report.

respectively Minister and First Secretary to the Permanent Delegation, whose co-operative attitude throughout this exercise has enabled the Committee to carry out this review.

## TABLE OF CONTENTS

| | | |
|---|---|---|
| I. | History of Australian Manufacturing Industry ....... | 5 |
| II. | Structure of Manufacturing Industry ............... | 11 |
| III. | Objectives of Industry Policy ...................... | 25 |
| IV. | Policy Framework and Instruments ............... | 29 |
| V. | Specific Industry Policies ......................... | 56 |
| VI. | Institutional Framework ........................... | 92 |
| Conclusions ........................................... | | 100 |
| Statistical Appendix ................................ | | 111 |
| Annexes ............................................... | | 139 |
| Bibliography .......................................... | | 172 |

# I

## HISTORY OF AUSTRALIAN MANUFACTURING INDUSTRY

1. Australian manufacturing industry parallels, in a number of important aspects, the manufacturing industry in other industrial nations, for example in its contribution to Gross Domestic Product (GDP), in its importance as an employer of labour and in the wide range of goods it produces. In other respects it differs significantly, particularly from the highly industrialized economies of countries like the United States and Japan.

2. The basic characteristics of the present structure of the manufacturing sector in Australia and the way in which they have developed are probably better understood and appreciated if examined in the light of their evolution. For this reason a brief outline of the historical development of the manufacturing sector is provided at the outset of this report.

3. The factors influencing Australian industrial development have been many and varied. The needs of the farming and mining communities gave the original impetus to industrial development. Physical factors such as a relatively small population spread over a large continent, a small domestic market and distance from the main world markets were significant, particularly in earlier years. Later, shortages and isolation during two world wars gave rise to further development. More recently, in the period of strong growth after World War II, particularly the 1960s, a high rate of population growth (resulting primarily from the Government's immigration programme), a considerable inflow of overseas investment and active Government encouragement, particularly through the tariff and other protective measures, greatly stimulated development.

4. A central feature in the development of Australian manufacturing industry has been the tariff. At the time of Federation (1901) it was an important issue providing lively debates between Victoria which had adopted a protective tariff to foster industrial expansion some thirty years earlier and New South Wales which has pursued a policy of free trade. At this time the manufacturing sector, mainly located in New South Wales and Victoria, was linked fairly closely to the needs of the primary sector and the immediate requirements of consumers with the typical manufacturing activities revolving around clothing, food and drink, agricultural machinery, woodwork, vehicles and fittings,

saddlery, books and printing. It accounted for something like 12% of GDP and employed around 17% of the workforce.

5. In the early years of Federation, tariffs were imposed by the Federal Government mainly for revenue purposes, but in 1908 protective tariffs were introduced to encourage local manufacturers. The move, in particular, raised duties on woollen goods, iron and steel and agricultural implements and was one of the first actions taken by the new Federal Government to stimulate industrial development. Another Federal initiative around this time was the introduction of a Manufacturers Encouragement Act (1908) which provided bounties for certain iron and steel products produced locally and which greatly assisted the embryonic iron and steel industry. By the outbreak of the first World War the manufacturing sector's contribution to GDP has increased to around 15%.

6. During the War imports of manufactured goods from the United Kingdom and western Europe were significantly reduced, emphasizing Australia's heavy reliance on manufactured imports. Shortages during the war period tended to limit industrial growth although the war years did provide a strong stimulus to the iron and steel and shipbuilding industries.

7. Following the cessation of hostilities the tariff was increasingly used to encourage industrialization which provided greater employment opportunities. In 1921 further tariff increases were introduced "to protect industries born during the war, to encourage others that are desirable and to diversify and extend existing industries". Chemicals, iron and steel and metal working were regarded as of key importance and given increased protection.

8. An important institutional development at this time was the establishment of the Tariff Board in 1921. It was created to provide the Government with independent advice on the level of protection needed by different industries. In broad terms its powers and responsibilities remained substantially unchanged for fifty years until it was replaced by the Industries Assistance Commission in 1973.

9. In the buoyant climate of the twenties the Australian manufacturing sector expanded strongly in association with increased capital inflow, immigration and further tariff increases. Growth was especially marked in the iron and steel, clothing, woollen textiles, electrical, timber (including furniture), glass and motor vehicle assembly industries. By the onset of the Depression in 1930, manufacturing was contributing around 18% to GDP.

10. With the introduction of emergency tariffs for balance of payments and employment reasons during the period 1929-31 and the devaluation of the Australian pound in 1931 import replacement industries were given a new impetus. Although the growth of manufacturing

was slower than in the 1920s, and in fact contracted in the early thirties, the volume of manufacturing production by 1938-39 was 15% above that in 1928-29, whilst the contribution to GDP was about the same as ten years earlier.

11. War-time mobilization, the imposition of import restrictions in 1939 and the difficulty of importing essential supplies stimulated the development of the engineering, machine tooling, aircraft, arms and ammunition, clothing, rubber and other strategic industries. On the other hand a number of industries were restricted in their development due to capital issues control and reduced consumer demand.

12. Although post-war expansion of manufacturing got off to a slow start because of shortages of imported plant, machinery and raw materials and local shortages of power and labour, manufacturing had commenced by 1950 a long period of sustained growth, stimulated initially by a high level of consumer demand and the 1951 Korean War commodity boom.

13. Over the last twenty five years output of manufacturing industry has more than tripled in real terms and has maintained its contribution to GDP in a time of dynamic growth in other sectors of the economy. It has been over this period that the Australian industrial profile has become more comparable with those of other industrialized nations.

14. Indeed the range and sophistication of Australian manufacturing industry has increased markedly since World War II. A feature of the development has been the establishment of major industries which either did not exist previously or had small pre-war foundations only, such as motor vehicle manufacture, oil refining, petrochemicals, paper, plastics and some non-ferrous metals. Significant expansion also occurred in the iron and steel, engineering and electrical industries. In contrast with the pre-war years when Australian industrial development was largely fragmented and diversified, the post-war period has seen the development of medium sized industrial complexes, many of which are integrated vertically and horizontally.

15. Post-war expansion was aided by a number of factors. The introduction of the Government's immigration programme in 1947 resulted in a rapid increase in population growth which provided an enlarged domestic market and increased workforce.

16. A heavy inflow of overseas investment brought with it new technology and skills, and has had an important influence on both the rate of development and diversity of manufacturing industry in Australia. It has been particularly significant in the more rapidly growing industries such as motor vehicles, petroleum refining, chemicals, petrochemicals, pharmaceutics, electronic equipment and man-made fibres.

17. Development during the 1950s was greatly assisted by the imposition of import restrictions which provided a considerable degree of

insulation from overseas competition. They were introduced for balance of payment reasons and complemented existing tariff protection. With the removal of import licencing in February 1960 the tariff again became the major protective device. For the first time in many years local industry was exposed to effective competition from overseas suppliers.

18. In this period there was considerable pressure placed on Australia's tariff making machinery. For example, in the year following the lifting of import restrictions, fifty five references were forwarded to the Tariff Board compared with thirty one the previous year. Also, in the early sixties, special legislation was enacted to enable temporary protection to be granted pending the receipt of a Tariff Board report.

19. The 1960s also saw a renewed emphasis on increasing the efficiency and productivity of industry and on seeking new markets overseas. During the sixties the Government introduced a number of measures to encourage Australian manufacturers to export, to stimulate indigenous research and development and to curb restrictive trade practices.

20. A number of significant factors including the resurgence of tariffs as a main influence on industrial and economic development, the gradual improvement in the overall balance of payments position, the discovery of new mineral resources and an increasingly tight employment situation, has led to a considerable debate in Australia in recent years on the aims and direction of tariff policy. In the latter half of the 1960s, for example, the Tariff Board began to look closely at the effects of tariff protection on resource allocation, and to question the adequacy of the traditional approach to tariff making which essentially revolved around the review of duties only in response to manufacturers seeking increased protection. It felt that a more systematic approach should be adopted to tariff making, including the development of criteria against which the desirability of encouraging different industries through the tariff, could be judged. Following this initiative by the Board, the Government in April 1971 decided that there should be a systematic review of the tariff, beginning with those industries having a relatively high level of protection and which had not been reviewed recently. The Government's present policies in relation to tariff protection will be explored in more detail in a later chapter.

# II

## STRUCTURE OF MANUFACTURING INDUSTRY

21. The previous chapter has highlighted the growth in the range and sophistication of the Australian manufacturing sector in the post-war period. Manufacturing production, employment and investment have changed continuously in the period but the sector has maintained its relative importance in terms of contribution to Gross Domestic Product. The tertiary sector, and in more recent years the mining industry, have exhibited the fastest growth rates whilst agriculture has declined in relative terms.

22. The position in 1971/72 of the manufacturing sector in the Australian economy might be briefly summarized in the following way. The sector:

- contributes 24% of GDP;
- employs 24% of the total workforce;
- accounts for 13% of gross fixed capital expenditure;
- supplies over 20% of exports;
- utilizes over 60% of all imports.

23. During the 1950s and the early 1960s the changing structure of the manufacturing sector reflected to a significant extent the growth of import replacement industries. While import replacement is a natural occurrence in the course of economic development it was greatly assisted in Australia by the policies adopted by the Federal Government, particularly those of tariff protection. However, in recent years the industries experiencing the highest growth rates have not been the so called import replacement industries. Despite the need for the various statistics to be interpreted cautiously it is noticeable that the growth in the value added, employment and investment in industry groups such as chemicals, petroleum and coal products, fabricated metal products, other machinery and equipment, and particularly textile, clothing and footwear has been below the total manufacturing average since 1968/69. * On the other hand, industry groups such as food, beverages and tobacco; basic metal products; wood, wood products and furniture have increased in relative importance.

* Most statistical comparisons in this Chapter and other parts of the report involve 1968/69 as a base year because in that year, the Australian Bureau of Statistics inaugurated a new series of census of manufacturing establishments which was not comparable with earlier censuses.

Location

24. The general distribution of the manufacturing workforce throughout Australia is shown in the map accompanying the statistical appendix. It will be noted that most of the population and consequently the workforce is located in a relatively small area of the country. This pattern which has continued in recent years reflects the increasing trend towards centralization and the mutual interaction between population growth and industrial expansion and also could be a direct reflection of industry having been located at or near major markets.

25. N. S. W. and Victoria, the most populous states, are also the most industrialized, accounting for 74% of both value added and employment in the manufacturing sector.

26. The current pattern of industrial production in the States is shown in table 2. 1. N. S. W. and Victoria dominate each industry group, with N. S. W. being particularly strong in basic metal products and chemicals, petroleum and coal products, while Victoria is rather more dominant in the textile, clothing and footwear group. The most important industries in Queensland, in terms of percentage of total "Australian value added", are the food, beverages and tobacco, and wood, wood products and furniture groups; whereas in South Australia the transport equipment industry is most significant.

Production

27. Australian manufacturing industry's present contribution of 24% to GDP, is comparable with a number of other industrialized countries, such as the United States, the United Kingdom and Canada but is somewhat below that of others, notably Japan and West Germany. Table 2. 2 outlines the contribution of manufacturing industry to Gross Domestic Product in a number of selected overseas countries.

28. In 1971/72 manufacturing industry contributed $ 8,558 million to GDP, which is more than double the figure of ten years before and represents an average annual growth rate of 8. 5%. With the overall economy growing at a slightly faster rate manufacturing industry's contribution to GDP has marginally declined during the period from a post-war peak of 26% of GDP reached in 1959/60 to 24% in 1971/72. This development is explained by the rapid growth of the public sector and the services sector, which have both progressed of an annual rate higher than the rate of the manufacturing sector. This evolution, compared to other industrialized countries, can be considered as normal. On the other hand, the mining sector has growth at a particularly rapid rate over the last few years thus contributing to the relative decline of the manufacturing sector in the economy. If one adds to these factors the strong growth of public expenditure announced in the 1974-1975 budget, the contribution of the manufacturing sector to

Figure 1

VALUE ADDED BY INDUSTRY GROUP 1972/1973

(Total = $ 10,750 m)

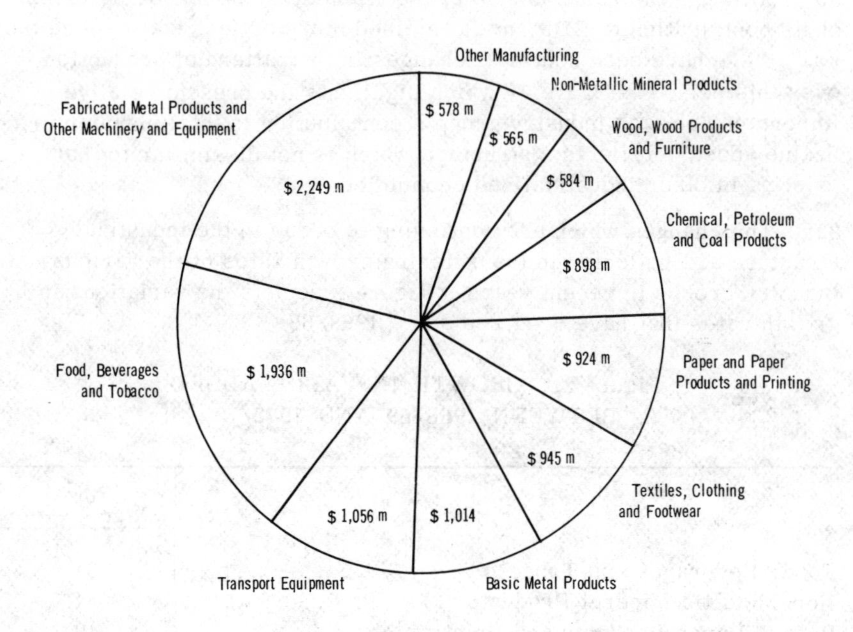

GDP may be expected to decline slightly in the forthcoming years, provided the economy as a whole grows at a quicker pace.

29. Official statistics are not available for the growth of manufacturing in real terms over this period. However, GDP has grown in real terms at an average annual rate of 5.4% over this period, compared with an average annual growth rate of 9.1% in money terms.

30. Although the relative size of the manufacturing sector in terms of its contribution to GDP, has remained more or less static since the war, there have been continual changes in the pattern of production over this period. Figure 1, which highlights the present relative importance of each industry group's contribution to total manufacturing "value added", reflects a structure which is not dissimilar to that existing in other industrialized economies.

31. The changes which are continuing to occur in the industrial structure are reflected in the differing growth rates of the various industry groups in recent years. Figure 2 depicts the variations in growth rates that have occurred since 1968/69.

Figure 2. GROWTH IN VALUE ADDED BETWEEN 1968/69 AND 1972/73

| | % |
|---|---|
| Food, Beverages and Tobacco | 64 |
| Non-Metallic Mineral Products | 54 |
| Paper, Paper Products and Printing | 49 |
| Wood, Wood Products and Furniture | 48 |
| Total Manufacturing | 44 |
| Chemicals, Petroleum and Coal Products | 42 |
| Basic Metal products | 39 |
| Fabricated Metal Products, Other Machinery and Equipment | 37 |
| Textiles, Clothing and Footwear | 33 |
| Transport Equipment | 26 |

32. The variations in the rate of growth of value added coincide, to a considerable degree, with those of employment and capital investment. For example, the food, beverages and tobacco group which led growth in value added in this period, has also increased its contribution to employment and capital investment at a faster rate than manufacturing as a whole. The relatively low growth in value added in the textiles, clothing and footwear group has occurred during a period in

which there has been a relative decline in employment and a falling off in the level of annual capital investment.

33. The factors contributing to the different rates of growth between industry groups are many and varied. Within the food, beverages and tobacco group, the strong growth in recent years can be attributed mainly to two factors. Firstly owing to a vagary in the statistical classification that has resulted in "abattoirs" being classified as a manufacturing operation, the dramatic increase in the export of fresh and chilled meat has been included in the manufacturing sector. The other major factor is an increase in the Australian standard of living which has been reflected in a rise in demand for non-essential non-food items such as beverages and malt and tobacco products (see table 2. 3).

34. The level of tariff protection would also appear to bear some relationship to growth rates (see table 2. 4). The analysis at this stage is somewhat crude and so undue emphasis should not be placed on the observable relationships between growth rates and levels of protection. However, bearing in mind all of the necessary qualifications and limitations it is interesting to note that on average, one may observe an inverse relationship between the level of protection in either nominal or effective rate terms and the growth rates in value added over the period. Thus the food, beverages and tobacco group with both the lowest average nominal and effective rate has had a relatively high growth whilst the clothing and footwear group with both the highest average nominal and effective rate has had a relatively low growth rate.

Employment

35. Manufacturing industry employs approximately 1. 3 million people or 24% of the total workforce. There has however been a slight decline in the importance of the manufacturing sector as an employer of labour since World War II. This has occurred during a period when its relative importance as a contributor to Gross Domestic Product has tended to remain relatively static.

36. The relative importance of the various industry groups as employers of labour is outlined in Figure 3.

37. Associated with the changing pattern of production in recent years, there has also been a change in the pattern of employment. Figures 4 shows the change in the total employment numbers by the various industry groups between 1968/69 and 1972/73.

38. A significant feature of the increase in overall manufacturing employment, has been the growth of female employment. In the period 1968/69 to 1972/73 the growth in female employment was just over 5%, compared with 3. 5% for total employment. The increasing importance of female labour has occurred in the following industry

Figure 3

EMPLOYMENT BY INDUSTRY GROUP, 1972/1973

(Total = 1 308 732)

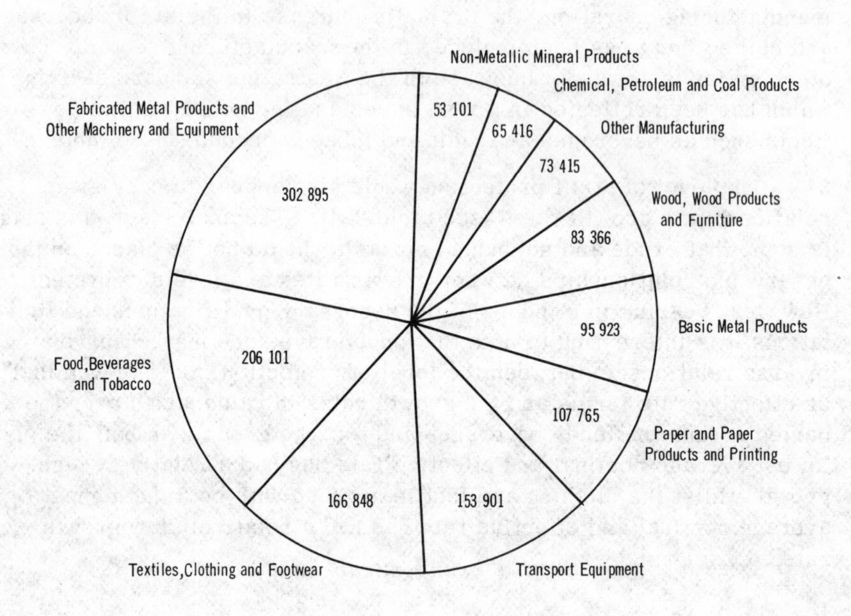

Figure 4. GROWTH IN EMPLOYMENT BETWEEN 1968/69 AND 1972/73

| | % |
|---|---|
| Food, Beverages and Tobacco ................ | 11. 5 |
| Basic Metal Products ........................ | 8. 7 |
| Transport Equipment ......................... | 6. 5 |
| Paper, Paper Products and Printing ........... | 6. 1 |
| Non-Metallic Mineral Products ................ | 3. 9 |
| Total Manufacturing ..................... | 3. 5 |
| Chemical, Petroleum and Coal Products ....... | 2. 6 |
| Fabricated Metal Products, Other Machinery and Equipment ............................. | 0. 7 |
| Wood, Wood Products and Furniture ........... | 0. 4 |
| Textiles, Clothing and Footwear ............... | -7. 7 |

groups: basic metal products; wood, wood products and furniture; food, beverages and tobacco; and transport equipment. Overall, the textiles, clothing and footwear group remains the most significant employer of female labour. A detailed outline of employment in manufacturing is given in table 2. 5.

39. Immigration policies of post-war Governments have played a major role in providing a labour force for manufacturing industry. Currently, immigrants account for approximately 40% of the total labour force in manufacturing, with their contribution in the Textiles, Clothing and Footwear Group being as high as 50%.

Labour Productivity

40. During the 1960s, increases in labour productivity in the manufacturing sector of 3. 6% per annum were somewhat similar to the increases in a number of other industrialized countries such as the United States, the United Kingdom and Canada, but below the increase in a number of other countries such as Japan, West Germany and France. (Table 2. 6 outlines the relative situation). This position continued into the early 1970s, although it would appear that for the latest year in which data is available there has been a strong improvement in the rate of productivity growth in Australia compared with other countries. Whether the 1972/73 figure represents a departure from past trends, or whether it reflects peculiarities in that year, will only be established when later data becomes available.

41. Published productivity indices for individual manufacturing groups have not been available since 1967/68. Estimates suggest however, that productivity gains have not been uniform throughout the manufacturing sector and show, for example, that the textile, clothing and footwear group has tended to enjoy an average annual labour productivity increase well in excess of the average for the manufacturing sector as a whole. By comparison, the metal manufactures, machinery and vehicles group has shown quite poor results.

42. These productivity results are interesting when compared to figures on growth in value added, employment, etc. The productivity increases in textiles, and footwear and apparel may be explained by increased capital intensity: whilst the annual capital expenditure per head rose to a peak in 1969/70, it subsequently declined to below the 1968/69 level.

However, during 1969/70 over 40 million dollars were invested in the industry as a result of quite significant machinery replacement policies adopted by the companies (see table 2. 7).

The relatively poor productivity results of the metal manufactures and machinery sector can be explained by the under-utilization of plant and equipment during the period under review. The industry had also suffered from power strikes, labour unrest and material shortages.

Capital Investment

43. The manufacturing sector accounted for 13% of gross fixed capital expenditure in 1972/73. Over the past decade, growth in private gross fixed capital expenditure in manufacturing has tended to be below that for the economy as a whole with mining and tertiary sectors of the economy dominating capital expenditure during the period.

44. Within the manufacturing sector, the basic metal products and food, beverages and tobacco groups were the areas of heaviest capital expenditure in 1972/73 as demonstrated in Figure 5.

45. There has been considerable variation in the growth of fixed capital expenditure between various industry groups in the period 1968/69 to 1972/73. The pattern in Figure 6 is similar to the corresponding diagrams for employment and value added and reflects the continuing change that is occurring in the Australian industrial structure.

46. Associated with the continued growth of capital formation in the manufacturing sector, capital intensity per employee has more than doubled over the last decade. This reflects the move by Australian manufacturing industry into both capital intensive industries and methods of production.

Figure 5

FIXED CAPITAL EXPENDITURE BY MANUFACTURING INDUSTRY

1972/1973

(Total = $ 1,256 m)

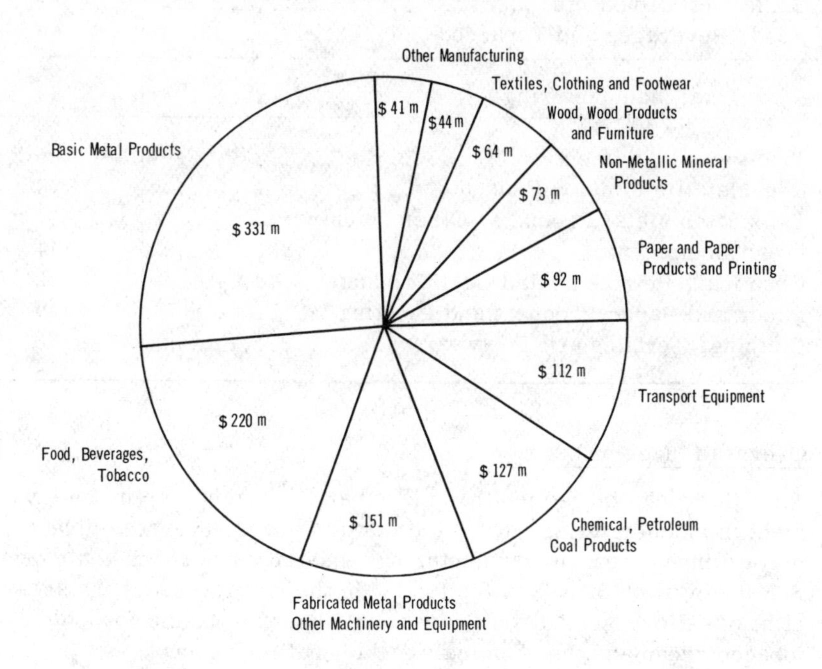

Figure 6. GROWTH IN FIXED CAPITAL EXPENDITURE BETWEEN 1968/69 AND 1972/73

| | % |
|---|---|
| Wood, Wood Products and Furniture ............. | 156 |
| Basic Metal Products ......................... | 89 |
| Food, Beverages and Tobacco ................... | 67 |
| Total Manufacturing ...................... | 39 |
| Transport Equipment ......................... | 25 |
| Non-Metallic Mineral Products ................. | 24 |
| Fabricated Metal Products, Other Machinery and Equipment ................................. | 14 |
| Chemical, Petroleum and Coal Products ......... | 12 |
| Paper and Paper Products and Printing ........... | 9 |
| Clothing, Textiles and Footwear ................ | -10 |

## Overseas Investment

47. Overseas investment has played an important role in the investment in manufacturing. Over the last ten years, overseas direct private investment in manufacturing industries has reached almost $ 2,000 million or 33% of the total. In the last few years the areas of heaviest overseas direct investment appear to be the food, drink and tobacco group and the chemicals and oil refining group.

48. Data on overseas control of Australian manufacturing industry is somewhat dated. In 1966/67, the last year for which statistical information is available, only 4% of factories in Australia were controlled by overseas interests. However, this relatively small proportion of factories accounted for more than a quarter of total value of production and about a fifth of average employment in manufacturing industry.

49. In that year, the degree of overseas control varied substantially between individual sectors (see table 2. 8) and it would appear that overseas control was highly concentrated in certain heavily capitalized and technologically complex industries - in particular motor vehicle construction and assembly, rolling and extrusion of non-ferrous metals and chemicals. In small scale industries where technology is less important or advanced (e. g. clothing), overseas control is much less significant. Over 90% of total foreign ownership was attributable to investors residing in the United Kingdom or the United States.

within this industry group and the opportunities that exist for efficient production at a low level of operation.

Overseas Trade

59. Manufacturing industry' contribution to total exports has continued to increase in recent years despite the growing importance of mineral exports. In 1972/73 manufacturing industry accounted for over 20% of exports compared with 12% a decade earlier. Currently, exports of motor vehicles and parts, and chemicals each account for around 16% of the total value of manufactured exports. The ranking of manufactured export products however, fluctuates from year to year and therefore annual figures can only be taken as a guide to the relative importance of individual products (see table 2. 13).

60. With regard to the pattern of exports by sector, one may note that, without being able to classify industrial sectors under the two categories (import replacement and export orientation) three sectors appear to be particularly export-oriented: basic metal products, textiles and food, exporting respectively, 19%, 12% and 10% of their turnover in 1968/69 (see table 2. 14). Two sectors have experienced a particularly rapid rate of increase of their export sales over the period 1963/64-1973/74: exports of chemicals (+31% p. a. on average) and on vehicles and spare parts (+21% p. a. on average) (see table 2. 15). In the case of chemicals, this development is due to a large extent to the growth of exports of alumina to the United States; in the case of motor vehicles, the growth is due to the rapid increase of exports to New Zealand, in the framework of a free-trade agreement between the two countries, and to South Africa, both these countries being the main customers of Australia for these products.

61. Markets for Australian manufactured exports mainly border the Pacific and Indian Oceans. The location of these markets differs markedly from those for total Australian exports and undoubtedly reflects the transport cost advantages that Australia has for areas close to its borders.

62. Manufactured goods represent around 80% (or $ 5,000 million in 1973/74) of total imports into Australia, with the United States, the United Kingdom and Japan being the main supplying nations. This indicates that despite the development of manufacturing industries in Australia, there is still a heavy reliance upon imports of manufactured goods. Imports of chemicals and textiles have shown markedly high rates of growth in recent years (see table 2. 17).

63. Not all manufactured imports are of finished products suitable for final consumption or use as capital equipment. Imports of producers' materials for use in manufacturing industry (excluding fuels and lubricants) currently amount to over $ 2,000 million and

account for around 38% of total merchandise imports. Most of these imports are already partially or completely transformed into the manufactured state. Since 1965/66 there has been a gradual reduction in the importance of imports of producers' materials for manufacturing industry compared to total imports (see table 2. 18). By comparison, imports of finished goods have played a relatively more important role.

# III

## OBJECTIVES OF INDUSTRY POLICY

64. The analysis and statistical data in the previous chapter have shown the importance of the manufacturing sector in the national economy. It underscores the fact that, as is the case in other industrialized countries, overall economic performance is significantly influenced by the performance of the manufacturing sector. Specific objectives which the Government has in relation to manufacturing industry are therefore very much influenced by, and indeed, should be seen as complementing a wider range of broad economic and social objectives, many of which are closely interrelated.

65. The Government's overall aims in managing the national economy, not only have a direct influence on industry itself through, for example, the application of monetary and fiscal policies, but also condition the more specific aims adopted in relation to the manufacturing sector.

66. The broad economic and social objectives of the Government have in fact been spelled out as policy guidelines for the functioning of the Industries Assistance Commission. Section 22(1) of the Industries Assistance Commission Act, a body established to advise the Government on matters affecting assistance to industry (see Chapter 5), states:

67. "In the performance of its functions, the Commission shall have regard to the desire of the Australian Government, in pursuing the general objectives of national economic and social policy and urban regional development, to improve and promote the well-being of the people of Australia, with full employment, stability in the general level of prices, viability in external economic relations, conservation of the natural environment and rising and generally enjoyed standards of living, and, in particular, to the desire of the Australian Government to:

a) improve the efficiency with which the community's productive resources are used;
b) encourage those economic activities in Australia, and the producers of the goods and services concerned, which contribute to improving the efficiency with which the community's productive resources are used;
c) facilitate adjustment to changes in the economic environment by industries and persons affected by those changes;

d) recognize the interests of consumers and consuming industries likely to be affected by measures proposed by the Commission;
e) ensure that any measures for assistance to, and development of, industries are integrated with national economic policy as a whole;
f) ensure that Australia's trade and protection policies are compatible; and
g) provide adequate scope for public scrutiny and evaluation of the basis of the Commission's reports."

68. In addition the Government in seeking to implement a range of social welfare programmes sees an improvement in real growth of the economy as a major means of implementing these programmes. Its economic policy including manufacturing industry policy, is therefore aimed at achieving improved resource allocation and consequently higher rates of growth resulting in a higher real Gross Domestic Product.

69. Industrial development, and the Government's attitude towards it, is also influenced by other broad socio-economic goals such as the desire to promote greater Australian ownership and control of Australian industry and resources, the preservation of the natural environment, securing a better deal for the consumer and improving the quality of life in the cities.

70. Against the backdrop of these broad economic and social strategies, many of which directly influence industry development, the Government has developed a number of more specific aims in relation to the manufacturing sector. Broadly these might be summarized as promoting a more competitive spirit in Australian industry, lessening its reliance on Government support and encouraging it to adapt and respond to change.

71. During his presentation to Parliament of the first annual report of the Industry's Assistance Commission the Prime Minister stated: "It is my Government's policy to improve the efficiency with which the Community's productive resources are used by encouraging those activities, those producers of goods and services who contribute to more efficient resource usage. We will not encourage those industries which place a disproportionate burden on the Community's resources. Our prime concern is for the needs of the community rather than those of particular industries. In order to assist employees and firms to make the necessary adjustment to desirable structural changes, we are implementing a comprehensive and generous adjustment assistance scheme."

72. With a commitment to improving growth in real income and realizing that Australia has limited resources and a small domestic

market, the Government believes that the best prospects for industrial growth, in the long term, are closely related to those areas in which Australian industry can specialize and compete internationally. This view represents a change in emphasis from the more traditional Australian attitude towards industrial development, which has tended to encourage the establishment and growth of import replacement industries. It should not be anticipated however, that the existing industrial structure, so much of which has developed as a result of traditional attitudes, is going to be changed overnight. Rather, the process of restructuring industry is seen as a gradual and developing one. Also, having so far defined the major direction it intends to follow with regard to the development of individual structures, the Government has not, at this stage, attempted to quantify in any way these orientations.

73. The Government recognizes that if movement of resources from one industry to another is to be achieve effectively, Government assistance will be required to actively promote and facilitate the mobility of labour and capital. To these ends, considerable effort has recently been devoted to the formulation and introduction of structural adjustment policies.

74. In addition, increased industrial efficiency and improved productivity are seen as having important roles to play in strengthening the competitive position of the manufacturing sector, and in increasing the growth of real income. The Government has therefore sought to improve both efficiency and productivity in a number of different ways. It has seen the need, for example, to tackle the problems facing small business; to encourage industrial research and development and, to promote the application of modern design, industrial processes and management techniques.

75. The Australian Government recognizes also the importance of the internal industrial environment as a measure of the personal well-being of employees and that personal job satisfaction is essential if overall industrial efficiency is to increase in the long term. This is, nevertheless, a relatively new area of emphasis and quite a lot of activity is or has been going on over the last eighteen months to two years.

76. As to labour participation in management, the Australian Government has recognized, within its own activities, the merit of direct involvement in management by representatives of workers and efforts have been made to ensure that there is adequate employee representation on Government Boards and Commissions and in all enterprises of significance to the economy. It is part of the Government's philosophy that those who are affected by Government decisions, are entitled to adequate consultations in the process of decision making. Considerable work and study has been going on in this subject, with reference particularly as to what other countries are doing in this field.

77. It is also the intention of the Government to become increasingly active in guiding future industrial policy and in so doing involve industry more frequently in the preliminary discussions leading up to the formulation of these policies.

78. As a major step towards stimulating interest in the formulation of industrial policy in Australia, as well as crystallizing various policy options, the Government has recently announced the formation of an expert committee comprising representatives from industry, government, the trade unions and academic circle to prepare a Green Paper on Manufacturing Industry Policy. The terms of reference for the Committee are:

> "To advise on appropriate policies for the development of manufacturing industry, including:
>
> 1) the machinery required for integrating such policies with the Government's general economic, social and regional policies;
> 2) the place of exports and imports in the development of manufacturing industry; and
> 3) the role of firms of overseas origin in manufacturing;
>
> and to advise on communication between the Australian Government and the private sector and the State governments with respect to the development and implementation of such policies".

79. The inclusion in the terms of reference of a section on communication demonstrates the Government's awareness of the need in the formulation and implementation of more efficient industrial policies, of an effort to integrate more closely industrial policy objectives with those of other areas of Government action. This interrelationship constitutes a constant source of potential conflicts and consequently trade-offs have to be made: first, among industrial policy objectives, and second, between these objectives and those pertaining to other policy areas.

91. The amount of revenue foregone in 1973/74 through the main taxation concessions to all industries (including manufacturing) is estimated to have been about $ 314 million (this estimate excludes a miscellany of lesser provisions because of lack of data or questions about the extent to which they may properly be regarded as wholly "industrial assistance"). The main provisions relating to manufacturing industry have been the investment allowance and various export market incentives.

92. In 1962 an investment allowance for manufacturing industry was first introduced into the taxation system in Australia. Provision was made for 20% of the amount of new investment in certain plant and machinery to be allowed as a once-and-for-all deduction from assessable income. This was in addition to the normal depreciation allowance. The policy measure was introduced during a period of recession with the aim of encouraging increased investment in industry. The concession was suspended at a time of more buoyant con itions, in February 1971, and was re-introduced a year later, a ain to stimulate investment. In August 1973 the measure was withdraw during a period of full employment of resources. The estimated cost t evenue in 1972/73 was $ 45 million and in 1973/74 it was $ 54 mil n.

93. An independent Committee of Enquiry investigated t effects of the investment allowance when the new Government came power (end 1972). The report produced by the Committee stated r alia "It has been argued in the past that the investment allowanc ovides a stimulus to investment which can be valuable for boosting conomy at a time of economic recessional slow-down. That of cours ld suggest the removal of the concession at other times such as present (1973) when the economy is coming under strain. The however, little evidence for the contention that the allowance is effective tool for countercyclical intervention of this kind. Man turing investment showed only a subdued pick-up in 1962 and 196 following the introduction of the allowance in 1962 and continued t fall sharply notwithstanding the restoration of the allowance in Fe ruary 1972 following its earlier suspension. At the present rates public company tax the subsidy conferred by the allowance is equiva lent to 9.5% of plant cost, which is unlikely to weigh heavily against the many other considerations which influence investment decisions, in particular, the outlook for demand for the product concerned. It would seem that broadly speaking most of the plant in respect of which the allowance is claimed would have been purchased anyway."

94. In both the 1973/74 and 1974/75 Budgets measures have been adopted that substantially reduce the extent of taxation and other concessions extended to particular sectors of industry.

95. The removal of certain subsidies for country areas which was announced in the 1973/74 Budget could be expected to have an effect on

manufacturing industry located in non-metropolitan areas. Among these subsidies were concessional postage rates on registered newspapers and periodicals, concessional telecommunications charges to the media and a system of low telephone rentals that has previously applied in non-metropolitan areas. In the same Budget, the Government increased the allowable margin between the wholesale price of certain petroleum products in metropolitan and the wholesale price in non-metropolitan areas by about 50% per gallon. Previously, a subsidy was paid to the petroleum industry to maintain a 3.3 cents margin and subsequently a 5 cents margin. At the end of July 1974 this was removed.

96. In the 1973/74 Budget the Government implemented a number of recommendations of the Task Force appointed by the Prime Minister to review the continuing expenditure policies of the previous Government including disguised expenditure through the taxation system. The abolition or modification of revenue concessions directly affecting industry (widely defined including primary manufacturing, mining and tertiary) are estimated to have led to a full year increase in receipts of over $ 300 million.

97. Additional fiscal measures have been introduced at times other than the Annual Budget; these include changes in the levels of indirect taxes, postal charges and social security payments. The Government is also devoting attention to the development of longer term budgeting through a system of forward estimates. As part of its policy to encourage sub-metropolitan and regional growth, telecommunication incentives to firms located in these selected centres are being actively considered to ensure that their distance from suppliers and markets does not severely disadvantage them.

98. In summary, policy towards industry is a subsidiary consideration in the general thrust of fiscal policy, but will sometimes be relevant in determining the vehicle for changes in policy. However, the Budget has a substantial influence on industry through the many direct and indirect forms of assistance that are extended, even though there has been a considerable reduction, in the latest two Budgets, in taxation concessions extended to particular sectors.

99. The current policies and programmes adopted by the Australian Government require an increase in the share of resources going to the public sector. Consequently the Budget can not be regarded as solely an instrument of short term demand management, but as also the major vehicle for implementation of the Government's social and economic objectives. While the 1973/74 Budget introduced a large increase in government expenditure, the Government was careful to avoid adding to net pressure on resources which were already under strain and the increase in outlays budgeted for was more than covered by increased receipts.

100. The levels of direct taxes on companies and of indirect taxes in Australia appear to be somewhat higher than the average in OECD Countries as a whole, while the level of direct taxes on households is somewhat less than the OECD average.

101. The structure and operation of the Federal Taxation System is being reviewed by a specially appointed Committee of Inquiry. The Committee was appointed to:

a) examine and inquire into the structure and operation of the Federal Taxation System; and

b) formulate proposals for improving this System either by way of making changes in the present system, abolishing existing forms of taxation or introducing new forms of taxation.

The following forms of taxation are being covered: Income Tax, Sales Tax, Estate Duty, Gift Duty, Duties of Excise imposed for the purpose of raising general revenue, and duties of Customs that correspond with duties of excise so imposed.

102. An interim report of the Committee has been submitted to the Government and was released in September 1974. Because of the wide definition of Taxation System adopted in the reference to the Committee, all sectors of the community including the manufacturing sector, will be affected in some way by any action taken by the Government based upon the Committee's report.

Monetary Policy

103. Because of the constraints on fiscal policy including the size of desired Government expenditure programmes, particular emphasis was given to monetary policy in restraining inflationary pressures during 1973 and 1974. The slow down in economic activity and deterioration in the employment situation in the second half of 1974 led to a change in the emphasis of monetary policy. Policy has recently been directed to ensuring that the immediate and basic needs of the economy for finance are met and accordingly there has been a significant easing in financial conditions.

104. Monetary policy in Australia since 1973 has made flexible use of the instruments available including open market operations, adjustments in the terms of Government loans, variations in the statutory reserve deposits lodged by banks with the central bank, and a number of exchange control measures designed to affect the cost and availability of overseas borrowings. In addition, legislation has been passed by the Australian Parliament for government regulation of financial corporations outside the banking system.

105. Although monetary policy basically has been used to achieve general economic management objectives, a number of considerations have led to measures to temper its impact so far as particular industries and activities are concerned.

106. For one thing monetary policy can have a disproportionate impact on certain sectors and general efficiency grounds suggest that these areas be protected from the full impact of policy. Secondly, because it has been claimed that financial markets unnecessarily discriminate against certain classes of borrowers, governments have established institutions catering for these groups. Given that the groups that find it difficult to raise finance tend to be the most vulnerable to a general tightening in policy, these two considerations are really different sides of the same coin.

107. At the present time the full impact of monetary policy is partially offset for the housing industry, agriculture, the export sector, local and semi-government bodies and certain other parts of industry.

108. A satisfactory level of activity in the housing industry always has been an important policy goal. Alterations to the asset ratio requirements of the savings banks and general lending directives from the Reserve Bank to the banks have enabled a separate policy on housing to be operated independently of the general stance of monetary policy. Australian Government payments to the States for welfare housing represent another important means of off-setting the impact of a tight monetary policy.

109. Other measures that have been adopted to protect housing from the full weight of policy include Budget allocations to savings banks for lending for housing, a tax rebate scheme in respect of mortgage interest payments (estimated cost $ 130 million for a full year) and the Housing Loans Insurance Corporation (which enables institutions like permanent building societies to extend the coverage of loans). More recently legislation has been passed by the Parliament setting up the Australian Housing Corporation which is empowered to carry out the Government's constitutional responsibilities in the housing field including direct loans to families for housing purposes.

110. Although much of the preferential treatment that exporters have traditionally received from the trading banks has been removed over recent years exporters still have access to special borrowing facilities. The Australian Banks' Export Re-Finance Corporation provides assistance to individual banks to enable them to handle very large or extended-term export transactions. The Export Finance and Insurance Corporation also assists certain groups of exporters in obtaining long-term credit to finance export sales.

111. Other industrial groups, especially small business concerns, have benefited from the Commonwealth Development Bank and the Term

Loan Fund of the trading banks. The Australian Resources Development Bank and the AIDC also provide finance and assist Australian enterprises to participate more fully in development projects.

112. The Financial Corporation Act, when operative, will widen the scope for the selective use of monetary policy.

113. In summary, the selective impact that monetary policy can have on the economy has always been a consideration. Measures have been taken and institutional arrangements established to ensure that certain more vulnerable groups and industries are not needlessly disadvantaged by policy actions designed to meet overall economic management objectives.

External Account

114. Two of the major economic problems facing the present Government when it came to power in December 1972, were a fundamental disequilibrium in the balance of payments and inflation. During calendar year 1972, for example, the overall surplus in the balance of payments was about $ 2. 2 billion and at the end of that year reserves stood at a record $ 4. 7 billion. In addition to fiscal and monetary measures, the Government has made flexible use of the instruments available on external account, including adjustments to the exchange rate, controls on the inflow of capital funds and the adjustment of tariff levels. Since December 1972 the Australian dollar has been revalued upwards twice and did not follow the American dollar when it was devalued in February 1973. In addition, an across-the-board reduction in non-revenue tariffs by 25% was made in July 1973.

115. A further major decision taken by the Government, which has had an indirect effect on industry, was the devaluation of the Australian dollar on 25th September, 1974.

116. The exchange rate changes and the tariff cuts prior to the devaluation, together with the other measures mentioned above, were directed specifically at the capital account and designed to bring about adjustments in the balance of payments to reduce Australia's excessive reserves and to increase the flow of resources to Australia. These measures were successful. The capital account turned around very quickly while the adjustments in the current account were more gradual. Substantial changes were apparent in the second half of 1973. There was in particular a very marked strengthening in the rate of growth of imports due to the specific measures taken to stimulate them but also to the very high level of internal economic activity. This very strong upward trend in imports, combined with the slower growth in exports, saw the current account of the balance of payments moving into a large deficit by the first half of 1974. In addition, domestic demand and production were also slowing down and the

Government considered some action was desirable to offset these developments. Since the post-Smithsonian revaluation of over 20% was partly a reflection of the essentially temporary increase in commodity prices, and not necessarily indicative of a permanent shift in the terms of trade or Australia's relative production potential, devaluing the dollar was considered to be the most reasonable alternative: the objectives were to slow down the rate of growth of imports (which had increased by 51% in 1973/74), to increase dollar receipts for exports and to remove a major barrier to capital inflow.

117. Decisions on exchange rates have to be taken primarily in the light of maintaining an appropriate balance in external payments. Bearing in mind the developments in Australia's balance of payments described above, it is clear that devaluation has no direct intended implications for competition policy. At the same time, one of the purposes of the devaluation obviously was to moderate the growth of imports to a more sustainable level. The Government has adopted a policy of industry restructuring mentioned earlier but it is seen as a gradual and developing process.

118. Industry will also benefit from the devaluation, but it should be remembered that industries subject to protection were, of course, affected by both the appreciation of the value of the dollar and the tariff reductions of July 1973. The depreciation will, therefore, only partly offset the appreciation, let alone the tariff cut.

119. Accompanying the above measures the Government imposed certain conditions on borrowing from overseas. A ban was imposed on borrowings from overseas for a term of less than two years which was reduced to six months in November 1974 and subsequently removed. For other overseas borrowings, a Variable Deposit Requirement (VDR) was introduced in December 1972 under which a proportion of the funds borrowed must be deposited without interest with the central bank. This percentage was initially fixed at 25%, then raised to 33 1/3% in October 1973, and decreased to 25% in June 1974. In August 1974 the VDR was reduced to 5% and later on to 0%. It is believed that capital expenditure on manufacturing industry has suffered as a result of this restraint, but to quantify any such effect is virtually impossible.

## Trade Policy

120. The development of significant levels of trade between Australia and the rest of the world has traditionally resulted from the continued success the export-oriented primary sector balanced by the need to import a wide range of capital goods and materials to develop and expand the manufacturing sector.

121. Since the end of World War II, the level of Australia's international reserves has had a significant influence upon trade policy.

Adverse current account balances coupled with low international reserves led to various short term measures such as quantitative and import restrictions designed to provide some relief for the balance of payments problems. These balance of payments problems were reversed in the early seventies with a surplus on current account of $ 608 million in 1972/73 (the first since 1956/57) and international reserves in the same year reaching a record level of $ 4,325 million, this level being over three times greater than the average level throughout the sixties. This development allowed the Government to adopt a series of policies designed to help reduce the internal problem of tight goods supply, to encourage the manufacturing sector into a restructuring of its operations so as to achieve a more efficient use of resources, and to limit the inflow and growing dominance of foreign capital in Australian industry. The policies adopted by the Government in response to this situation have been outlined above. These policies were the main contributors towards the 1973/74 current account deficit of $ 707 million and an overall balance of payments deficit of $ 678 million as measured by net monetary movements.

122. Within the broad framework of the national economic and social objectives, there are two major aspects of trade policy which have direct effects on manufacturing industry, viz:

i) the need to contain imports led to the development of a broadly based industrial sector, and
ii) the encouragement of increased exports of manufacturers to help reduce reliance on the primary sector.

123. The key instrument used to achieve the first objective has been the tariff, with relatively limited use being made of subsidies. As mentioned above, however, import licensing has been used in the past for balance of payments reasons and often, indirect beneficial effects for industry have occurred.

124. An independent source of advice on tariffs has been available to the Government since 1921 when the Tariff Board was established. Recently the role of the Board was expanded under legislation establishing the Industries Assistance Commission (IAC) so that now all sectors of industry and all types of assistance are open to the analysis of an independent body.

125. Achievement of the second objective mentioned above, that is increasing exports of manufactures, involves two main policy instruments - the Export Market Development Grants Scheme and the Export Bank.

126. With a small domestic market, it is often difficult for Australian industry to attain economies of scale and thus be able to reduce unit costs. Also the small size of the domestic market limits the degree of competition facing Australian industry and thus hampers the development of new skills and technology and impedes innovative economic

activity. Consequently in order to open a wider and more competitive market and reduce Australia's dependence on primary exports, policies have been introduced to encourage manufacturing industry to seek export markets.

127. The two export incentive schemes which operated for several years up to 30th June, 1974 were the Market Development Allowance, and the Export Incentive Grants Scheme. The Market Development Allowance (MDA) was a taxation rebate of up to 42.5 cents for each dollar expended on export market development. The rebate was in addition to any deduction allowable for the expenditure under the provisions of the Income Tax Assessment Act. The MDA, by providing a measure of income tax relief, was designed to encourage exporters and potential exporters to incur promotional expenditure in advance of export sales and build up methodical and regular selling arrangements to ensure continuance of sales. On the other hand, the Export Incentive Grants Scheme provided for a rebate of payroll tax based on employment activity in production for exports which was granted in relation to increased levels of export sales achieved by a firm in any one year over and above the level in a moving base year.

128. The new Export Market Development Grants Scheme replaces the previous export incentive arrangements. It will run for five years from 1st July, 1974 with provision for review after 3 years and is particularly designed to encourage new and established exporters to seek out and develop overseas markets and to participate in Australian Government sponsored trade promotion. Under the Scheme, taxable grants will be payable on export promotion expenditure in respect of any exports of substantially Australian origin.

129. With regard to export financing, the Australian Government reconstituted on 1st February, 1975 the Export Payments Insurance Corporation (EPIC) to enable it to function as an export financing agency. The new body, known as the Export Finance and Insurance Corporation (EFIC), is responsible for both the functions of EPIC and the new export financing arrangements.

130. The Export Payments Insurance Corporation was originally established in 1956 as an independent statutory authority to provide a specialized range of insurance and guarantee facilities against the risks of non-payment not normally obtainable from commercial insurers. In performing this function the Corporation is required to operate on a commercial basis and to pursue a policy directed towards securing sufficient revenue to meet all its expenditure properly chargeable to revenue. The Corporation is fully guaranteed by the Australian Government.

131. EFIC, either as agent for the Australian Government or on its own account, also offers insurance cover on certain kinds of Australian

investment overseas. Indemnity obtained from EFIC covers such things as transfer blockages and expropriation and loss due to war and civil disturbance.

132. The decision to create an export financing facility followed an examination of existing credit facilities available to Australian exporters and the identification of a gap in the provision of funds at the medium and long term end of the market compared with Australia's competitors in international markets. The Export Finance and Insurance Corporation provides export finance for exports of machinery and capital equipment sold on medium and long term credit and for the establishment of lines of credit, especially to the developing countries and to state trading organisations.

133. Continued support for multilateral arrangements and participation in bilateral trade agreements, together with the measures outlined above are expected to ensure continued growth in the levels of manufactured goods exports with concomitant benefits for all sectors of the economy.

## Manpower Policy

134. The general aims of Australia's manpower and employment policies since 1945 have been the maintenance of full employment, the promotion of maximum utilization of available labour resources, and the efficient allocation of those resources. During the past 30 years economic policy has aimed at maintaining the highest level of employment consistent with reasonable price stability and adequate levels of international reserves.

135. In the past the means of achieving manpower objectives have focussed upon aggregate demand and supply forces in the market, the control and management of total demand through monetary and fiscal policies and the use of the immigration programme to overcome pressure caused by shortages in critical areas of the labour market.

136. Essentially, manpower planning in Australia has, in the past, been to settle on broad policy objectives and to influence the market mechanism where necessary so that its operation will achieve the desired result. To some extent this has been necessitated by constitutional limitations on the Australian Government's power to intervene directly in respect of labour, wages and prices.

137. Some areas of Government policy have had an important effect on the size and composition of the labour force. Among these have been the introduction of large scale immigration, the rapid expansion of the industrial base, the development of the Commonwealth Employment Service and activities designed to upgrade the skills of the labour force.

138. Changes in the economy's requirements for labour resulting from changes in economic conditions, technology or specific Government policies may result in restructuring the industrial labour sector. Programmes of assistance to employees include counselling, employment and training assistance. In respect of those adversely affected as a direct result of prescribed structural changes resulting from Government actions, additional adjustment assistance measures are available. These measures provide financial assistance with relocation, where appropriate, and maintenance of income for retrenched employees for up to a maximum of six months.

139. Under Australia's Constitution Australian Parliament's power to deal with industrial relations and wages is limited. Its principal power derives from a section of the Constitution which authorizes it to make laws with respect to conciliation and arbitration for the prevention and settlement of industrial disputes. The Central Government's powers are restricted to enacting legislation for the purpose of conciliation and arbitration and may, therefore, be termed a dispute type of power. At the federal level, the Australian Government intervenes in national wage cases and certain other major policy cases which are likely to establish general standards for the purpose of putting submissions to the Australian Conciliation and Arbitration Commission* on the merits or otherwise of the claims submitted by the parties.

140. Concerning the question of influence on wages, the Government proposed to National Employer and Union Representatives an arrangement at a conference convened by the President of the Conciliation and Arbitration Commission. The Government's proposal envisaged the reintroduction of automatic quarterly adjustments of wages for price movements; in other words, indexation on a percentage basis up to the level of average weekly earnings and an equal flat rate adjustment thereafter on wages which are higher than the average. As part of this proposal there would be an agreement by the Unions that for the duration of the arrangement there could be no further adjustment of wages for price increases; in other words, it is a conventional indexation proposal which has been under consideration.

141. The Conciliation and Arbitration Commission announced its findings on the indexation question on 30th April, 1975. In its decision the Commission did not recommend the automatic quarterly adjustments of wages for price movements as proposed by the Government, but said "it is our present view that the Commission should be unfettered to decide each quarter the form by which consumer price Index adjustments should be made and we invite comment on this procedure. Experience may show that changes need not take place as frequently

* For further information on the ACAC, see annex.

as each quarter." This view represents a substantial qualification to the principle of indexation as seen by the Government and unions.

142. In 1974 the Australian Government established the National Employment and Training System (NEAT), designed to cover more than just the previous employment training programmes, in its aim ultimately to retrain one per cent of the work force every year. The purpose of NEAT is to help alleviate unemployment, to increase the overall level of skill of the Australian labour force, to help overcome shortages of skills in the labour market and to remedy imbalances in labour supply/demand in particular sectors of industry. The development of manufacturing industry should be promoted by the retraining system as redundant labour resources will be directed towards areas most requiring skilled workers. It is expected that in its first year more than 18,000 people will enter training under NEAT.

143. Manpower policy now and in the future is aimed at enabling the Australian economy, including manufacturing industry and its workforce, to have a quick and flexible response to changing goals and circumstances.

## Competition Policy

144. It is the Government's aim to promote the efficient use of the community's productive resources with competition being regarded as the motivating force in the Australian economy. It is believed that strong competition will bring about healthy, efficient industry. The Government has therefore sought to encourage a competitive environment for domestic industry not only through its trade policy but also through its internal policies. Domestic policies aimed at increasing competition between firms concentrate on prices and pricing practices (i) by eliminating restrictive trade practices and (ii) by keeping a close watch on price increases.

### i) Trade Practices Legislation

145. Trade Practices legislation has been in existence since December 1965. However, a bill to strengthen considerably the existing law has recently been passed by Parliament. The provisions of the new Act differ substantially from the previous legislation in providing for stronger, more comprehensive and more effective control of restrictive trade practices.

146. The 1974 Act has been largely modelled on United States law, particularly Section 1 Sherman Act, Sections 3 and 7 Clayton Act and the Robinson Patman Act. The provisions have however been adapted in certain respects to suit Australian conditions.

147. The legislation has been presented by the Government as a measure to control restrictive trade practices, promote efficiency and competition in business and to counter inflation.

148. The main difference between the two pieces of legislation is that anti-competitive practices are to be directly prohibited by the new legislation itself whereas the general position under the previous Act was that an anti-competitive agreement or practice could only be prohibited for the future if it was found by a Trade Practices Tribunal to be contrary to the public interest and was then restrained by order. This case-by-case examination procedure proved time consuming and it was not possible to deal with more than a small proportion of agreements and practices in existence.

149. There is provision, however, for the granting, in appropriate cases, of clearances and authorizations to engage in certain practices or to proceed with mergers that would otherwise be prohibited. These authorizations include those cases where action taken to rationalize industry is condoned by the Government and is therefore not seen as being against the public interest by the Tribunal. The Act prohibits the following practices: contracts, arrangements or understandings in restraint of trade; exclusive dealing; anti-competitive mergers; resale price maintenance; monopolizations and price discrimination. There was no provision in the previous legislation for any control over mergers. As well as encouraging more competition in the economic system, there are stringent provisions relating to consumer protection in the Act. Together these measures can be expected to have a significant effect on business practices. However, as the Act was only passed in August 1974 it is too early to predict what the results will be.

ii) Prices Justification Tribunal

150. The Prices Justification Tribunal commenced operation in August 1973, with power to inquire and report to the Government on whether existing or proposed prices for goods or services, charged by companies subject to the legislation, are justified and, if not, what lower prices would be justified. The initial legislation provided that all companies incorporated in Australia whose revenue was $ 20 million or more in the preceding financial year were required to notify the Tribunal of proposed price increases and of proposed prices for new products or services. Inquiries into these proposals could then be initiated by either the Government or the Tribunal. The Tribunal has power to exempt, on the basis of a number of criteria, certain companies from the requirement of notifying intended price increases.

151. When the prices justification legislation was first introduced to Parliament, in May 1973, the Government stated that the measure was but one element, though an important one, in a broader strategy to help control inflation. The Government indicated that there was scope for firms (and particularly for large firms) to adjust prices without adequate discipline by the market. Given that situation it considered that the prices justification measure would improve the functioning of the market.

152. In August 1974 Parliament enacted legislation which is intended to strengthen the Tribunal and extend its scope in certain ways, particularly in the area of retail prices and prices of imported goods. The new Act removes the $ 20 million turnover restriction for inquiries made by the Tribunal, either at its own discretion or as required by the Government. The limit remains, however, insofar as it concerns the obligations by companies to notify price increases. The Tribunal will thus have greater power to inquire and report into prices charged by companies, irrespective of their turnover. The Tribunal will also be empowered, as an alternative to stating that it does not intend to hold an inquiry in the case of a particular proposed price increase, to notify the company concerned of any lower prices that it considers to be justified. The company concerned will then have 7 days to notify the Tribunal whether it accepts this lower price or prefers to proceed to public inquiry.

153. The Tribunal by 30th June, 1974 had received some 5,400 notifications of price increases and initiated 23 public inquiries. In addition, in some 400 cases proposed price increases have been reduced by companies without public inquiry after initial discussions with the Tribunal. In no case has a company proceeded contrary to the findings of the Tribunal. The legislation establishing the Tribunal does not contain any enforcement provisions.

154. The Statute does not lay down any criteria and the Tribunal has discretion in both the choice of criteria and the application to any particular case. There has been quite an amount of pressure in Australia seeking to have some definition put into a criterion that the Tribunal may use. But the Tribunal reiterates that it is a justification tribunal not a price control authority and that circumstances which may justify a price rise in one case may not be a justification in another case.

155. The Government recognizes that the operations of the Tribunal affect business profitability and subsequently the level of private investment. Accordingly in November 1974 the Government wrote to the Tribunal stating that, in light of the existing economic circumstances, it should give particular attention to the problems of sustaining and stimulating an adequate level of private investment and of maintaining rates of return on capital sufficient to induce the new investment required to maintain economic growth and employment.

156. The Tribunal's activities to date have certainly resulted in proposed price increases being reduced or delayed. Some of the commodities concerned have been products (such as steel) which are used as inputs by manufacturers, as opposed to being consumer products; and to this extent the Tribunal has clearly lessened the cost pressures on certain manufacturing industries. On the other hand it is conceivable that, by holding down returns to a manufacturer

on some of his activities (viz. , those which the Tribunal has powers to investigate), the Tribunal's actions might lead the manufacturer to turn to activities less useful, in the long run, to the community as a whole.

iii) Parliamentary Joint Committee on Prices

157. The Committee, comprised of members of both Houses of Parliament, was appointed in April 1973 to inquire and report to the Parliament upon:

a) complaints arising from prices charged by private industry and the public sector,
b) movements in prices of goods and services in particular sections of private industry and the public sector, as measured for example, by price indices, and
c) such other matters relating to prices as may be referred to the Committee by resolution of either House of Parliament.

158. Whilst the Committee possesses no mandatory powers, it does provide a forum at which members of the public, consumer groups, producers and other interested organisations can present opinions on prices knowing that the matters can be investigated and reports made to Parliament. The Committee also provides a readily accessible means by which the Parliament can be informed of problems on prices that might require Government action in the public interest.

159. At the time of writing the Committee has presented eight reports to Parliament and is presently inquiring into a number of other matters. Even though it has no direct power over prices and pricing policies, it is expected that the Committee's activities will have a modifying effect on undesirable pricing policies.

160. Both the Prices Justification Tribunal and the Parliamentary Joint Committee on Prices act through persuasion as opposed to action through control or sanction. The Federal Government has no power to control prices, such powers falling under the exclusive competence of State Governments. A referendum carried out in 1973 and designed to extend the power to control prices to the Federal Government failed to obtain the necessary number of favourable votes.

## Foreign Investment Policies

161. In recent years there has been a considerable shift in government policy regarding foreign investment, brought about by a number of factors. A consequence of earlier policies which attached great importance to encouraging a steady inflow of overseas capital was that a large part of certain sectors of the economy, particularly manufacturing and the extraction of minerals, came under foreign ownership or control. Surveys by the Government Statistician for the years 1962/63 to 1966/67 revealed that the value of production in manufacturing

enterprises under overseas control increased from 22.4% to 26.3% over this period.

162. The significance of these figures was heightened by the fact that foreign ownership and control was very much higher than this in a number of important manufacturing industries, such as motor vehicles, rolling and extrusion of non-ferrous metals, oil refining, chemicals and pharmaceuticals.

163. A further important factor was the change in the significance of investment flows for the Australian economy. Australia had long been accustomed to running a substantial deficit on current account. In recent years, however, the deficit has declined and the balance on current account became a surplus in 1972/73 for the first time since 1956/57.

164. This development occurred at the same time as a sharp increase in capital inflow with a resultant tripling of international reserves (from $ 1,511 million to $ 4,816 million between December 1970 and December 1972). The resulting increase in liquidity added to the problems of monetary management and of containing various inflationary pressures.

165. In response to growing concern over these problems the previous Government initiated a review of all aspects of overseas investment which led to the passing of the Companies (Foreign Takeovers) Act in 1972. This reassessment of Foreign investment policy was carried on after the Labor Government took office in December 1972.

## Foreign Takeovers

166. The general principles on which the Australian Government's policy is based were enunciated in a statement by the Prime Minister which was tabled in Parliament on 7th November, 1973. The Government believes that foreign investment, in partnership with Australian capital, must continue to play a significant role in Australia's economic growth. However, the policy of the Government is to adopt a more selective approach towards foreign investment than hitherto. The Government intends to ensure that foreign capital inflows are associated with productive investment which adds to Australia's real resources and brings benefit to the nation. The policy is being applied in a pragmatic way and cases are examined on their merits. There are no rigid rules regarding the required percentage of participation by Australian interests. Specific proposals are, however, examined in the light of the Government's general objective of promoting Australian control of its industries and resources, and of maximizing Australian ownership compatible with the degree of participation which Australia's general rate of savings can support. Account is taken of all the likely technological, employment, environmental, social and other effects of a proposed investment. The Government treats foreign

investment from all countries equally. The general policy applies to foreign investment in most industries; but, the Government also has a number of specific sectoral policies.

167. There have been no special or particular positions taken by the Government on foreign investment in manufacturing industry. Rather, proposals are examined on a pragmatic, case by case, basis in accordance with the principles outlined in the preceding paragraph.

168. On 19th December, 1974 the Government announced that it proposed to introduce new and comprehensive legislation for the control of foreign takeovers of Australian businesses. The previous Government had introduced foreign takeover controls on 26th September, 1972 and had partially incorporated these controls into interim legislation.

169. The new legislation will enable the Government to examine all takeovers of Australian businesses by foreigners and to prohibit such takeovers found to be against the national interest. A "takeover" will be a transaction which results in a change in the identity of the person in a position to determine the policy of an Australian business. An "Australian business" will be any private sector activity carried on in Australia in anticipation of profit. "Foreigner" will be defined to include a company incorporated in Australia where it is owned as to 15% or more by a single foreign interest or associated group or 40% or more by any number of foreigners and where the Minister is satisfied that the company is in fact foreign controlled.

170. The new legislation will enable the Government to examine:

a) an acquisition by a single foreigner or associated overseas group of an interest of 15% or more, or by any number of foreigners of an aggregate interest of 40% or more of the share or assets (including mineral rights) of a business;
b) splitting by an overseas interest of a substantial shareholding in a business where this involves an increase in voting rights;
c) acquisition by an overseas interest of a lease or licence over the assets of business;
d) an execution by Australian and/or overseas interests of an agreement which would give an overseas interest, which controls 15% or more of a business, the right to increase its proportionate representation on the board or management committee of the business concerned; or a change by a business in its articles of association or the terms of any memorandum, agreement or trust deed to provide for, permit or facilitate increased proportionate representation by a substantial foreign shareholder in the business on its board or management committee of a business; and

e) acquisition of shares or assets of a business incorporated in an overseas country where such transactions would result in a change in the control of the business concerned and where either 50% or more of the assets of the latter business are held in Australia or where the Australian assets of the latter business amount to more than $ 3 million.

171. All examinable transactions will be subject to the provisions of the new legislation. However, the Government will continue the existing administrative practice of intervening in takeovers of businesses with total assets of $ 1 million or less only in special circumstances.

172. Notification of takeover proposals will be examined by the Committee on Foreign Takeovers for report to and decision by the Treasurer. The Committee comprises representatives of various Government Departments. Proposals will be examined against criteria laid down by the Government. The principal criterion is whether the takeover will lead to sufficient net economic benefits to justify a change in control of the business concerned.

173. The new Act will empower the Treasurer to delay the implementation of foreign takeover proposals, to prohibit such proposals found to be against the national interest, to order divestiture of shares or assets acquired without due notice having been given or in contravention of orders and to apply to the Courts for the imposition of penalties.

174. On 12th June, 1974 the Prime Minister announced the establishment of a new Interdepartmental Committee, known as the Foreign Investment Committee, to examine and provide advice on foreign investment proposals which come under notice through the exchange control mechanism and do not involve the takeover of Australian businesses. The Committee has purely advisory functions. It parallels and complements the Committee on Foreign Takeovers.

175. The Committee has also been asked to bring forward, for the Government's consideration, detailed proposals for the screening of foreign investment activities which do not involve exchange control approvals - e. g. , investment proposals which would be financed by foreign interests from funds available within Australia.

## Industrial Development Funding

176. Capital has for many years been a scarce resource in the Australian economy. The increasing size of projects associated with new or expanding industrial ventures and the development of mineral resources has exacerbated that shortage in recent years. Successive governments have recognized the need for an institution outside the normal banking system which could marshall capital for the funding of industrial expansion.

177. In 1960 the Commonwealth Development Bank of Australia was established. The Bank's main function was to provide finance for primary production and for the establishment or development of industrial undertakings, particularly small undertakings. The Bank also provides advice and assistance with a view to promoting the efficient organisation and conduct of primary production or of industrial undertakings.

178. In fulfilling its lending function the Development Bank provides finance which is not otherwise available on reasonable and suitable terms and conditions. The Bank supplements, but does not compete with, other banks or sources of finance. The finance it provides is in the form of long-term loans and equipment finance under hire purchase arrangements. It is primarily concerned with an enterprise becoming, or continuing to be successful, and does not necessarily have regard to the value of the security available. It aims at increasing the output and improving the structure of primary and secondary industries, placing major emphasis on projects that will increase productivity through more efficient use of resources. The major part of the Bank's activities have, however, been concerned with primary industry.

LOAN APPROVALS AND ADVANCES OUTSTANDING

$ million

| | LOAN APPROVALS 12 MONTHS TO JUNE | | ADVANCE OUTSTANDING 30th JUNE | |
|---|---|---|---|---|
| | INDUSTRIAL | TOTAL | INDUSTRIAL | TOTAL |
| 1972/73 | 12. 7 | 41. 3 | 36. 8 | 235. 3 |
| 1973/74 | 12. 1 | 66. 1 | 38. 8 | 242. 3 |

179. Industrial loans outstanding to various sectors at June 1974 were: foodstuffs and preservatives $ 8. 1 million, engineering $ 5. 9 million, building materials and fittings $ 2. 7 million, electrical and allied manufacturing $ 1. 5 million, chemical products $ 1. 1 million, other manufacturing $ 3. 4 million, transport, storage and communication $ 1. 0 million, and other non-rural industry $ 15. 1 million.

180. A further development occurred in 1967 when the Australian Resources Development Bank (ARDB) was incorporated as a private company. Although the ARDB is owned by the seven major trading banks, its formation was strongly encouraged and aided by the Federal Government. The Bank's main function is to refinance trading bank loans for large scale projects in minerals, oil and natural gas. The Bank's capital funds are provided by the Reserve Bank (40%) and the shareholder banks (60%).

private entrepreneurs or individuals. As it becomes increasingly difficult to obtain access to the facilities offered by the city, it is the people who are least able to pay who suffer most.

189. For many years State Governments have pursued policies of decentralization, for example by providing incentives to manufacturing firms to set up in, or move to, non-metropolitan areas. Examples of incentives offered at present are: loans at favourable interest rates for land acquisition, factory construction and purchasing capital equipment, rail freight concessions; subsidies towards moving, housing and retraining employees; and (in Victoria) the rebate of State payroll tax. Generally these programmes are not selective either as to geographic location (provided, of course, the firm is not setting up within the metropolitan area) or as to the industry within which the firm works. That is, the programmes have as their main object the encouragement of location or relocation of manufacturing industry away from the capital cities. Evidence suggests, however, that the effectiveness of these policies has been limited for several reasons: adherence to a policy of non-selective decentralization, competition between States for industrial development and the absence of disincentives for industrial location in metropolitan areas.

190. Under the Constitution, the Australian Government has no power to levy locations-specific taxes or pay locations-specific subsidies and this restricts its ability to directly pursue some regional policies and programmes. An agreed programme of assistance between the States and the Australian Government could be arranged by grants or loans under Section 96 of the Constitution. Possible alternative methods of providing assistance on a locational basis would be open to legal challenge in the High Court and therefore subject to a degree of uncertainty.

191. Since December, 1972 significant moves have been made by the Australian Government towards a comprehensive national strategy for urban and regional development. Previously, although many activities of the Federal Government had an important impact on urban development there was little recognition of its responsibilities in this field, the task falling primarily to State and local government.

192. At this stage, a broad national strategy is emerging where the emphasis is on both selective decentralization to create alternative urban choices for Australia and provide greater equality of opportunity, and on improving the efficiency and living conditions of existing metropolitan areas.

193. An important objective in the national urban strategy is to foster a well balanced regional employment base. In the past the concentration of private sector investment in heavy industry in areas outside the capital cities failed to include a commensurate provision of female

employment opportunities. Many country towns also suffer from the lack of adequate range and depth of employment opportunities, and this has often been a major factor in their demise. A wide diversity of industry is necessary to provide a range of job opportunities and it also contributes to the economic stability of the area.

194. One important way of improving large urban areas is the development of sub-metropolitan centres to reduce the dominance of central areas and to distribute employment and service opportunities more equitably. In addition, metropolitan growth centres beyond the metropolitan fringes are being developed with a full range of employment, service and cultural opportunities and good access to the rest of the metropolitan region. Restructuring of the metropolitan areas is consistent with significant market trends in the location of industrial activity within large cities which, in recent years has resulted in the dispersal of many firms from central to suburban locations.

195. Support and encouragement is also being given to a limited number of carefully chosen regional growth centres or "new cities" which have the potential for accelerated development. * A policy of focusing on only a small number of urban growth centres will lead more quickly to the establishment of viable growth points needed to achieve a satisfactory diversion of population and economic activity away from existing metropolitan areas.

196. In most of these centres, however, manufacturing industry will be a major factor in creating the necessary employment opportunities to enable rapid growth to proceed as planned, although tertiary industry is playing an increasingly important role in the Australian economy, and for the prospects of these regional centres. It is recognized as important that the manufacturing establishments locating in growth centres (or elsewhere in decentralized locations) are likely to be economic and efficient in the long run, thus providing employment and growth in the area into the indefinite future without the need for long term subsidization.

197. A comprehensive Industry Location Policy for the Australian Government is still in embryonic form. Only segments of these policies are in operation and these only for a short period of time. Co-ordination of inter-governmental machinery is recognized as an urgent matter requiring early attention, and negotiations are being conducted at present to this end.

198. Associated with the decentralization strategy is active involvement by the Australian Government, in co-operation with the State Government, in encouraging the development of regional industrial

* e.g. ALBURY-WODONGA which is a large centre between Sydney and Melbourne.

complexes based on the exploitation of Australia's natural resources. In general terms, it is intended that these complexes should be located either close to the resources on which they will be based or close to an economic source of energy; that each complex should be significantly integrated in an input-output sense so as to maximise external economies; and that the complexes will increase the level of Australian processing of export products, particularly minerals.

199. Foreign organisations will participate in both the construction and operating phases of development and it is likely that local capital will have to be supplemented with overseas capital (both equity and loan funds). Three of the proposals which are currently under consideration may be of interest. Firstly, the Pilbara Scheme - preliminary investigations of this scheme have revealed that the establishment of some industries based on local resources, such as iron ore, natural gas and solar salt in the region, can be classified as profitable. Based on the assumptions on which the feasibility study was predicted, it would appear that petro-chemical and chemical-based industries would be the most attractive ones in that area. While the preliminary study has indicated some preferred sites for industrial development in the Pilbara region, at this stage alternative locations outside the region have not been investigated.

200. A second development project being investigated at the moment is the Bowen Basin Coal Complex in central Queensland. A preliminary study has revealed that an industrial complex based on local coal resources is technically feasible. However, at this time the study has not looked at the question of economic and marketing aspects. Further studies are currently under review at this point of time but the best prospects that are to be looked at will be iron and steel, aluminium smelting, metallurgical coke, caustic soda and chlorine power generation and coal processing to produce synthetic crude oil liquid fuels and chemicals.

201. A third development in another part of Australia, i. e. in South Australia is the proposed Redcliff petrochemical project located about 320 kilometres north of Adelaide. Partners in the Redcliff Petrochemical Company are ICI, Alcoa and Mitsubishi of Japan. The proposal is based on the production of ethylene from natural gas liquids produced in the Cooper Basin of South Australia, and of Chlorine and caustic soda from salt produced locally. Principal products would be caustic soda, to be used in Australia in alumina production, ethylene dichloride partly for local consumption, but mainly for export in the early years, polyethylene and components for blendings into gasoline. The South Australian Government at this point of time is seeking from the Australian Government loan finance for infrastructure, in particular for a power station, pipelines and domestic housing. Other important aspects, such as prices for fuel and feedstocks, pipeline charges, still remain to be finalized before the economics can be finally available.

202. The increase in and the size of the industrial complexes, i. e. for the local further processing of raw materials, does raise in the immediate future a question with regard to the possible co-operation of consumer countries in the financing of these complexes, and in the longer term the question concerning their impact on the industrial structures of Australia and the consumer countries. (For further details on the Australian Government's policies concerning this aspect of industrial development and the encouragement of treatment and fabrication of mineral resources in Australia, see Annex.)

203. In view of the comparatively limited size of the Australian market, and of the need to attain, wherever possible, full economies of scale, it is likely that these regional industrial complexes based on the exploitation of Australia's natural resources will be primarily export-oriented.

204. The concept of further processing of Australia's natural resources is in accord with the Government's policy of encouraging the treatment and fabrication of mineral resources in Australia and moving from being primarily an exporter of raw materials to becoming a substantial exporter of semi-processed and processed materials. This view was emphasized by the Prime Minister when he said in November 1974 that the Government's objective is the maximum level of mineral processing consistent with the rational use of Australia's resources.

Environment Policies

205. Environmental matters are to a significant degree State and local government responsibilities as the States have responsibility for land use management and industrial development within their boundaries. Nevertheless the Constitution does provide the Australian Government with the opportunity to exert influence over the environment policies of the States. For example, the Australian Government does have control over international trade and can impose conditions on financial grants it makes to the States.

206. Two policies of the Australian Government that have particular relevance to industry are the adoption of the Polluter Pays Principle (PPP) as enunciated by the OECD and the introduction of an environmental impact assessment procedure.

207. The basic objective of the PPP is to treat pollution control costs as part of the costs of production so that the costs of pollution control are reflected in the price of a particular good or service. Charging for the use of the environment will lead to an improved allocation of resources within the economy. Firms will restrict the use of the environment as it becomes more costly, while higher prices for goods produced by polluting industries should reduce demand for these products.

208. In an endeavour to ensure that environmental considerations are given proper consideration in decision making the Government has adopted the environmental impact statement technique. This technique is designed to ensure that environmental factors are considered equally with financial, engineering and other technical considerations when a decision is made on a particular proposal. It requires that before certain decisions are taken an impact statement should be prepared. The statement will be required to set out the need for the proposal, the objective of the proposal, the alternative means of reaching that objective and the environmental effects of these different alternatives.

209. Through the Environment Protection (Impact of Proposals) Act 1974, the Australian Government requires the preparation of impact statements for all proposals which are likely to have a significant effect on the environment and in which it has some involvement, e.g. export controls.

210. The procedures the Australian Government is adopting will provide that, except in unusual circumstances, impact statements will be made available to the public for its comment before they are finalized. In some cases this will involve public hearings. Most of the State Governments are also introducing the environmental impact statement technique although in some instances they will apply the technique in a different manner to the Australian Government.

211. Proposals affecting industry are, of course, the subject to the impact statement requirement. It is anticipated that this will result in a greater environmental awareness on the part of those in industry and those in Government responsible for industrial policy. The requirement will ensure a more thorough and broader evaluation of a proposal and will mean that in many instances environmental problems inherent in a proposal will be identified at an early stage so that changes in plans can be effected or remedies developed at that stage.

212. The use of the technique could also have an important influence on the siting of major industrial projects and the anti-pollution standards that are required to be observed.

# V

## SPECIFIC INDUSTRY POLICIES

213. In any examination of specific industry policies in the Australian context, it is desirable to start with tariff policy, which, although being part of trade policy, has also been the major Government method of influencing the structure and development of Australian manufacturing industry, particularly since the removal of import licensing in 1960. An examination of the policy is therefore essential in providing an insight into Government objectives for manufacturing industry.

### HORIZONTAL POLICIES

#### i) Tariff Policy

214. Australia's long-standing tariff policy is to accord reasonable and adequate protection against import competition to economic and efficient production. This policy was first clearly stated in the United Kingdom-Australia Trade Agreement of 1932. In the Agreement, Australia undertook to ensure that tariffs "shall not exceed such a level as will give the United Kingdom producers full opportunity of reasonable competition on the basis of the relative costs of economical and efficient production" with "special consideration to industries ... not fully established". In addition, the Agreement called for the affording of protection only to "industries which are reasonably assured of sound opportunities for success".

215. Since 1921, the Government has sought the advice of an independent body before deciding upon the level of assistance to be granted to particular industries. As mentioned earlier, the independent body is now the Industries Assistance Commission which replaced the previous body, the Tariff Board, on 1st January, 1974.

216. The actual criteria used by the Board in advising the Government on tariff policy have been gradually evolved over the years, particularly in relation to the interpretation of the central concepts of economic and efficient production. Efficiency was defined in a technical and managerial sense of combining inputs to produce output at least cost, given the economy's set of factor prices. The more abstract concept of "economic" was interpreted as meaning the provision of benefits - variously listed as direct and indirect employment, saving of foreign exchange, location in non-metropolitan areas,

defence, etc. - at not too high a cost in relation to the prices of imports. Implicit in the explanations was some notion of an upper limit to protection, beyond which it would not be reasonable to go.

217. In a major reconsideration of tariff criteria, set out in its 1966-67 Annual Report, the Tariff Board spelt out in some detail an essentially new approach to setting tariffs. Pointing to the complex structure of the tariff that had emerged from an ad hoc approach to tariff setting, and the overly diversified and fragmented industrial structure that it supported, the Tariff Board indicated that in future, it intended to consider requests for tariff assistance in the light of benchmarks or points of reference. Under the Tariff Board's points of reference approach, industries requiring effective rates of protection above 50% are considered to be high cost for Australian conditions, and need to provide evidence of generating above average external benefits if they are to be assisted at the level required for existence. Industries requiring effective rates of protection less than 25% are considered to be low cost and worthy of support.

218. In its 1973-74 Annual Report, the IAC estimated that the average effective rate for manufacturing industry in 1969/70 was 35%. This falls between the bench mark levels that the Board has previously delineated as high and low in that they said that about 50% effective protection was high, between 25 and 50 was medium and below 25 was low. The average rate should have been subsequently reduced by various decisions to lower tariffs since that time and more importantly by the 25% across the board tariff reduction implemented in July 1973. There is no mention of the points of reference bench mark criteria in the Industries Assistance Commission's First Annual Report, though there is quite an extensive discussion of high and low cost industries. This may mean that the IAC is moving away from a rigid adherence to the bench mark criteria.

219. The advantages of the "points of reference" approach for tariff setting is that it gives a clear meaning to the criterion of economic production, it facilitates greater consistency in decisions and it reduces uncertainty for businessmen considering investment in activities requiring tariff protection, by providing a guide to the likelihood of obtaining or retaining tariff support. It should result in greater specialization in areas of comparative advantage, hence improving the efficiency of factor use, and raising the rate of growth of per capita GDP. The thrust of the principles are towards the improved allocation of resources within the manufacturing sector, rather than the balance of resources between the manufacturing sector and other sectors of the economy.

220. By the mid-1960's there was a growing awareness of the problems associated with the then current approach to tariff setting of examining the protective requirements of industries or parts of

industries on a case-by-case basis in response to requests by particular industries for increased protection. A proposal for a progressive and systematic review of the Tariff to help remedy the problems associated with an essentially reactive approach to tariff setting was made by the Tariff Board in its 1966-67 Annual Report. The Board suggested that it should examine the main areas of production where there had been no recent public inquiries. It suggested that the sequence of the review should be established primarily on the basis of the height of protection but would take into account such matters as the size of industries and their interdependence. In this connection the Board said that it intended to publish in its next annual report a list of protected industries classified into high, medium or low cost production. The Board drew particular attention to the need to review Chapter 84 of the Tariff (dealing with machinery and mechanical appliances) during the progressive review.

221. The Board said that the basic reason for such a review would be to ensure that, in the future, the operation of the Tariff was more fully and consistently related to the Government's economic objectives. The main means of achieving this would be by improving resource allocation in the manufacturing sector by encouraging the development of, and the flow of new investment into, the more economic activities within the protected sector.

222. Following these recommendations the Government decided to refer portions of Chapter 84 of the Tariff to the Board. By June 1968 five references covering important sections of Chapter 84 has been referred for review. Early in 1971 the Government decided that a systematic review of the whole Tariff should be undertaken, along the lines which had been suggested by the Tariff Board in its annual reports. A further ten references relating to Chapter 84 of the Tariff were sent to the Board in May 1971 as part of this review. In April 1972 the Government announced that the tariff review programme would be advanced in order to be completed by 1978.

223. The extent and timing of the review references have been framed in consultation with the advisory body. These references leave it open to the advisory body to recommend any form of assistance which it considers appropriate. It is open to the advisory body to comment on the effects of its decisions on industries other than those immediately under reference to the extent that vertical and horizontal independencies are not covered by the reference under consideration. A list of the inquiries initiated mainly following suggestions by the Tariff Board and the Industries Assistance Commission is set out in table 5. 1. This table shows that such inquiries cover approximately 50% of value added in manufacturing industry.

224. The majority of references currently being dealt with by the Commission relating to manufacturing industry are those associated

with the progressive review of the Tariff and tariff revision references not arising from temporary assistance action. While it is true that a number of mandatory references have arisen as a result of Government action taken on Temporary Assistance Authority reports these represent only a relatively small part of the overall work of the Commission. Irrespective of the origin of references the Commission in all its inquiries applies a consistent set of principles which reflect the guidelines provided in the Industries Assistance Commission Act.

225. A significant recent development that has occurred in the way the Industries Assistance Commission operates is the decision by the Commission in the case of the report on the aluminium industry to publish a draft report. The draft report will provide the basis for a further public inquiry at which the individuals and firms interested in the report will be able to debate the Commission analysis and draft recommendations. The Commission will then in the light of the public inquiry finalize its report to the Government. The draft report procedure is a positive step by the Commission which should ensure that all relevant facts are brought out. If generalized it will represent a significant step away from the Tribunal-like nature of the Commission towards greater dialogue with industry.

226. Since 1960, a provision has existed for the imposition of temporary duties if urgent action is considered necessary. Temporary protection may, however, only be imposed after inquiry and report by a Temporary Assistance Authority and after the question of normal long-term assistance to the industry has been referred to the Industries Assistance Commission for inquiry and report. Such protection may only operate for three months following the receipt of the IAC's final report.

227. An integral element of the Australian tariff system is the by-law system which is a provision allowing protective duties to be waived in respect of goods, if such action would not penalize local manufacturers. In general terms by-laws are granted, under the authority of the Minister for Police and Customs, on goods for which suitably equivalent locally made goods are not reasonably available. Around 25%, by value, of total imports enter duty free under by-law. The existing by-law system is currently under review and it is envisaged that a Green Paper canvassing arguments for and against by-law, and alternative systems of concessional entry, will be published by the Government in the near future.

228. Provision is also made for the imposition of dumping duties. The object of this legislation is to protect local industry against discriminatory pricing practices. In 1973 the Government decided to bring Australia's anti-dumping legislation into line with the GATT Anti-Dumping Code and new legislation has recently been brought down in Parliament.

229. The present Government continues to support the key element of previous Governments' tariff policies, namely that, tariff policy should facilitate the optimal use of resources, whilst ensuring that adequate account is taken of resultant economic and social effects. Additional policies have been developed over the past eighteen months to give assistance to those individuals and firms affected by such change.

230. One significant recent policy decision relating to tariff levels, but not primarily a function of Government tariff policy, was the across the board 25% tariff reduction in July 1973. The action was designed to restrain price increases, by increasing competition and stimulating, in the shortrun, a flow of additional imports to help meet pressing demand. However, the Committee which recommended the change observed that the tariff reductions envisaged will encourage investment to concentrate more on those economic sectors where long term national prospects are relatively more promising.

231. In addition to that tariff cut, there had been a number of other quite major tariff decisions taken in Australia, e. g. the rates on a number of goods were decreased significantly: consumer electronics, domestic appliances, heating and cooling equipment, earth moving and construction material, handling equipment, fibre containers and paper and textile bags. Since the institution of adjustment assistance for the 25% tariff cut and subsequently the SAA* programme statistics have been kept of the number of persons claiming to be retrenched as a result of the Government's tariff actions prescribed for the purposes of these schemes. A comparison of retrenchments due to structural change with total unemployment (see table 5. 2) from all sources makes it clear that prior to the commencement of the general cyclical downswing in mid-1974 retrenchments due to structural change were extremely small both absolutely and in relation to total unemployment. Subsequent to mid-1974 retrenchments due to structural change, resulting from in particular rapidly growing imports, rose in step with total unemployment.

232. In response to the imposition of temporary restrictions on a range of imports new registrations of retrenchments due to structural change have fallen considerably since December 1974; the number of people unemployed as a result of structural change still awaiting placement has fallen since January 1975. Over one hundred firms have now applied for closure compensation under the structural adjustment assistance programme. Three quarters of these applicants were in apparel and textiles, while the rest were in footwear and electronics and metal manufacturing.

* Structural Adjustment Assistance.

233. The Government, in introducing the measure, recognized that increased import competition could affect production and employment in Australia and accordingly, introduced special adjustment measures for employers and employees affected by the reduction. These are discussed later in this chapter.

234. The tariff has been, and will no doubt continue to be, an important instrument in guiding and supporting industrial growth. It will continue to be an important element of the Government's general economic policy directed towards the achievement of economic growth, full employment, increasing productivity and rising standards of living. However, it is likely that assistance provided by the tariff, will tend to be more even-handed than has been the case in the past. That is, the dispersion (and hence complexity) of the tariff will be reduced as the Tariff Review proceeds. The international trend to greater exchange rate flexibility, and the willingness of the Government to develop instruments to achieve directly the objectives which the tariff achieved indirectly (e. g. location of industry), will further reinforce a general tendency for the level of protection to fall. This tendency may also be reinforced by Australia's participation in the forthcoming multilateral trade negotiations, and by pressures arising from the increasing export interest being shown by, and capacity of, manufacturing industry. The net result is likely to be a re-allocation of resources from high cost to lower cost activities, greater specialization both within and between industries, and ultimately, a higher rate of growth of per capita GDP due to more efficient use of resources.

ii) Industries Assistance Commission (IAC)

235. The Prime Minister when introducing the IAC Bill in Parliament said:

> "We propose to extend to all Australian industries a system of assistance which, for the last 50 years, has applied only to manufacturers, through the Tariff Board ... the Board is an independent statutory authority which has an advisory function only. It has no executive role. The essence of the Tariff Board system is that it makes public inquiries and public reports on questions of assistance for industry referred to it by the Government. The Government proposes to extend this system to industries in other sectors of the economy because it believes the system has, over a long period, proved its value to successive governments in an important and difficult area of government decision-making."

236. The primary function of the IAC is to advise the Government on the nature and extent of the assistance which should be given to individual industries in the primary, secondary, and tertiary sectors of the economy. This intention is conveyed principally in Sections 21 and 23 of the IAC Act part of which reads as follows:

"The functions of the Commission are to hold inquiries and make reports ... in respect of matters affecting assistance to industries and other matters that may be referred to the Commission ... ".

The Commission is, in essence, an advisory body. The IAC Act does not oblige the Government to accept the Commission's advice; final responsibility for assistance matters lies with Parliament, not the Commission.

237. Of the 389 reports presented by the Tariff Board between 1st January 1961 and 31st December 1973, 355 were adopted without change. However in the same period, of the 63 reports covering important industries (defined as industries employing over 1,000 people) the recommendations contained in ten were not accepted in full and in eleven cases references sent to the Tariff Board included policy directives. Since taking office in December 1972, the present Government has accepted the advisory body's recommendations except in five cases. *

238. The most important part of the IAC Act relates to the so-called mandatory provisions whereby matters of assistance must be referred to the Commission before Government action can be taken. Section 23(3) states that action shall not be taken to provide assistance to a particular primary or secondary industry or to a particular group or groups of primary or secondary industry unless a report has been obtained from the Commission. Included under the mandatory provisions are import duties, import restrictions, financial assistance beyond two years, and financial assistance for a period not exceeding two years where, as a result, an industry will have received financial assistance for more than two of the last six years. Explicitly excluded from the mandatory provisions, are bilateral and multilateral trade agreements and tariff preferences for developing countries.

239. The IAC Act also provides for a Temporary Assistance Authority separate from the Commission. The function of the Temporary Assistance Authority is to inquire into, and report on action necessary to protect an industry, from imported goods, pending receipts and consideration of a report by the Commission in relation to those goods. The Temporary Assistance Authority (TAA) can recommend assistance by means of a temporary duty or temporary prohibition on imports, or a combination of both measures. Temporary assistance cannot operate for more than three months following receipt by the Government of a report by the IAC on a reference which must include the tariff items

* The five cases not accepted by the Government relate to: Cathode Ray Tubes, Domestic Appliances, Consumer Electronic Equipment, Calcium Carbide and Passenger Motor Vehicles. In three of the above cases the Government amended the Commission's recommendations, in another, consideration of the Report was deferred, and it rejected the report on Passenger Motor Vehicles.

benefiting from the temporary assistance. Referral to the IAC of such references is mandatory.

240. In a letter to the Prime Minister during November 1974 the Chairman of the IAC informed the Government that during periods of unemployment the Commission would not recommend the immediate implementation of changes in assistance likely to cause temporary disruption to employment. Under this approach the IAC, when considering recommending a long-term level of assistance that may lead to changes in employment in an industry, now includes in its report on the industry a supplementary recommendation to apply in the short-term. This supplementary recommendation is designed to ensure that acceptance of the Commission's report does not add to existing employment difficulties in the industry concerned.

241. An important effect of this new approach is to separate short-run consideration, arising from cyclical fluctuations in the economy, from long-run objectives of industry development policy. This leaves the Government free to deal with questions on long-term assistance in a way which promotes the long-term welfare of the community as a whole. It also removes the likelihood of attempting to settle questions of long-term assistance in response to the pressures arising from short-term changes in the economy.

242. The Government may refer to the Commission a broader range of assistance matters than those which are mandatory. The Commission also has the power to initiate its own inquiries into industries that have not been reviewed for ten years (in the case of import duties), or six years (in the case of other forms of assistance).

243. When referring a matter to the Commission, the Government may specify a period within which the Commission is to report on that matter. If the Commission has not reported within thirty days of the expiry of the specified period the Government may take action without receiving a report.

244. The Commission also has to report annually to the Government on its operations and as far as practicable, report on the general range of assistance provided to industries by the Government, and the effect of that assistance on the development of assisted industries and the economy generally.

245. The policy guidelines set out in the Industries Assistance Commission Act described in Chapter 3 make explicit the kinds of general considerations that have in the past formed a basis for the Tariff Board's deliberations. Their presence in the IAC Act does not, consequently, require the Commission to modify the "points of reference" approach developed by its predecessor, the Tariff Board.

246. The Commission currently consists of nine full-time Commissioners and 18 Associate Commissioners. Legislation increasing the

number of Commissioners to eleven is currently before Parliament. In order to give the Commission maximum flexibility, and to draw on people of the highest calibre, there is no limit on the number of Associate Commissioners that can be appointed. An Associate Commissioner may be appointed for the duration of a particular enquiry or for a period not exceeding five years.

iii) Adjustment Assistance

247. The decision to implement adjustment assistance programmes is relatively recent. In February 1973, the Government established an Interdepartmental Committee (IDC) to advise on measures to facilitate desirable structural changes in the Australian economy. The 25% tariff cut was introduced however, before the IDC report was received and an interim adjustment assistance programme was therefore introduced. The programme included assistance to both employees and firms suffering "serious injury" as a result of the tariff reduction. A one-man tribunal was established to determine questions of eligibility and to recommend the most suitable type of assistance.

248. Following consideration of the Interdepartmental Committee's report, the Prime Minister announced on 23rd April, 1974 the details of a permanent programme of adjustment assistance.

249. In setting up this permanent programme, the Government acknowledged that optimum economic management, from time to time, necessitates actions which require resources to move from one use to another. Such transfers of resources are necessary to accommodate the Government's industrial, urban, regional, defence and technological goals.

250. The basic purpose of the structural adjustment programme is to promote and ease the process of desirable change by providing various incentives. It aims also to ensure that if the changes are desirable in the national interest, the nation and not the individuals affected should share the costs involved.

251. An important aspect of the scheme is that the special adjustment assistance measures are not available in all situations arising from Government action; but only for those actions, or events, which the Government has specifically stated as being those for which adjustment assistance is to be made available. At the time of writing the measures apply in respect of nine decisions, the 25% tariff cut of July 1973, the Consumer Electronics tariff decision, the Domestic Appliances tariff decision, the lifting of quota on woven shirts and knitted outergarments, Dairy Industry Adjustment, the Shipbuilding Decision of December 1973, Passenger Motor Vehicle and Component decision, the Woven Man-Made Fibre Fabrics tariff decision and the removal of sales tax exemption on Aerated Waters. The available measures are described below.

Assistance for Employees

252. An employee who is unemployed as a direct result of a structural change, for which the Government has prescribed adjustment assistance, and who has obtained a statutory declaration from his employer to this effect, is eligible for the following assistance:

- income maintenance equal to the employee's average weekly earnings excluding overtime for the previous six months (up to one and a half times national average weekly earnings) for a period of up to six months,
- retraining, relocation assistance or early-retirement benefits (details of the latter form of assistance have yet to be finalized).

253. Administration of the scheme is flexible enough for owners of small-scale enterprises forced to cease operations, because of a prescribed structural change, to be treated as employees, if they wish.

Assistance to Firms

254. Assistance to firms is to be administered by a Structural Adjustment Board. The Department of Manufacturing Industry is administering the scheme in the interim until the Board is established.

255. In the case of firms, the structural change must have adversely affected, or was adversely affecting, the firm to the extent of rendering a significant part of its assets incapable of economic production or the desired change must be unlikely to occur at a reasonable speed and reasonable economic cost without assistance to the firm. Secondly, the firm is required to take reasonable steps for self-help but it must be unlikely that the firm will be able to complete adjustment through its self-help measures, e. g. a firm may not be able to obtain finance on normal or reasonable terms and conditions. And thirdly the generally available measures in the economy have to be utilized to the full but have to be inadequate. Once these eligibility criteria have been satisfied the firm is eligible for:

- consultancy grants (on basis of 50% consultancy cost up to a maximum of $ 10,000),
- loan guarantees,
- closure compensation (on basis of 85% of the difference between the written-down value of assets for taxation purposes and realized sales value).

256. In the case of closure compensation the eligible firm has to have closed down and sold its assets before compensation is paid. For consultancy grants and the loan guarantees, specific proposals associated with restructuring have to be put forward. Assistance under the programme is not of a continuing nature. It is envisaged as a single specific payment or guarantee to a particular firm. Moreover there is a set period, normally one year, during which applications, based on a prescribed cause, have to be lodged.

257. As yet the scheme has been operating for an insufficient time to make any real assessment of its results. However, the following information indicates the extent to which the assistance measures have so far been called upon. By the end of February 1975 over 22,000 individuals had applied for income maintenance. By the middle of March 1975 more than 600 enquiries had been received from firms for information while 221 had submitted formal applications for assistance. These were in the following fields: milk processing, apparel, textiles, footwear, electronics, engineering, domestic appliances and shipbuilding. Of these formal applications, excluding the milk processing, where the application arose from the termination of the free school milk scheme, about three-quarters were for compensation relating to full closure.

258. The Government has set up an interim committee with the immediate role of advising the Government on practical problems associated with applications for assistance under the scheme until the Structural Adjustment Board is established.

259. In announcing the formation of the interim committee for structural adjustment, the Deputy Prime Minister said that the adjustment assistance programme was an innovation in Australian industrial policy and, accordingly, the government intended to approach the problems of adjustment in a flexible way. The introduction of the regional employment development scheme and the special assistance to non-metropolitan area programme are two examples of the government's desire to avoid personal hardship in the short-term, whilst seeking to pursue more efficient use of resources in the longer term.

260. The regional employment development scheme is designed to improve opportunities in areas of excessively high unemployment by encouraging local initiatives in these areas to develop suitable work programmes. The scheme is, of course, part of an overall manpower policy and, as such, is not aimed directly at industry but does have a considerable indirect effect. The special assistance for non-metropolitan areas programme was announced by the Prime Minister on 22nd October, 1974 and is aimed at alleviating, quickly and effectively, short-term problems of industrial unemployment in country towns. Under the scheme, direct financial assistance, additional to the existing policies, is available to manufacturers in country towns which have been adversely affected by structural changes such as tariff cuts or the removal of import quotas. The programme is also intended to play an important role in the government's longer-term policies for improving the structure of Australian industry and ensuring sound and worthwhile regional development. The financial assistance primarily takes the form of direct payment of subsidies to manufacturing firms for sustaining or phasing-out of existing production and employment. If necessary, pre-payment of the subsidy in a lump sum to assist in providing

immediate liquidity for firms will be considered. Assistance would be conditional on the firms participating in industry restructuring wherever possible. The programme also includes provision for capital grants to firms or local bodies for the establishment of new viable alternative production and employment opportunities in non-metropolitan areas. Finance may also be provided for feasibility studies into restructuring for new production facilities.

261. The adjustment assistance programmes are quite a new development for Australia and it is perhaps too early to judge whether they are sufficient to deal with the sectoral problems caused by import competition. As has been indicated the Government has found it necessary to introduce certain changes to its adjustment assistance programmes. In spite of these changes however, the changing economic situation together with the practical experience of administering the various programmes has revealed certain problems and anomalies. The Prime Minister accordingly announced on 7th April, 1975 an urgent review of the Government's schemes for the maintenance of income and employment and also allied schemes for structural adjustment to employers.

iv) Industrial Technology and efficiency

262. The Government recognizes the importance of the introduction, dissemination and development of modern technology in industry. With this in mind, it has reviewed or is currently reviewing existing schemes to ensure that such programmes provide greatest support to areas with the greatest need and promise.

263. The Government's overall programme for improving the innovative and technological capability of industry takes a number of forms:

i) infrastructural provisions;
ii) specialized incentive schemes; and
iii) general aids to industry including managerial efficiency aids.

Infrastructural Provisions

264. An environment conducive to the development of modern technology is provided by the infrastructural provisions contained in the legal, taxation and educational systems. Such provisions include patents, copyrights and trade marks, various taxation deductions for expenditure associated with research and development and appropriate educational facilities.

Incentive Schemes

265. The principal incentive scheme, and for that matter the principal specific policy, designed to encourage industrial innovation and technological capability is the Industrial Research and Development Grants Scheme. The Scheme was introduced in July 1967 to operate initially for a five year period. It was subsequently extended

with certain modifications in August 1972 for a further five years. Further amendments were made in 1973.

266. The broad objective of the scheme is to promote the development of efficient Australian industry, by providing an incentive to manufacturing and mining companies to allocate more of their own funds to systematic research and development activities, as a means of developing new, and improving existing, products and processes. Eligibility for grants extends, broadly speaking, to manufacturing and mining companies incorporated in Australia and conducting such activities in Australia, in the relevant grant year or the succeeding grant year.

267. Two types of grants are available, viz; general grants, applying to eligible expenditure up to $ 50,000 in a grant year, and selective grants, on that component of eligible expenditure in excess of $ 50,000 made in accordance with a number of broad national interest criteria specified in the legislation namely - the development and use of Australian physical resources; the expansion of export: import saving and improvement of the ability of Australian products to compete with imported products: the improvement of productivity and reduction of costs in Australian industry: and the development of the Australian economy in a manner conducive to the defence of Australia. It is worthy to note, however, that while these criteria are employed in determining the elegibility of firms to receive selective grants, applications for such grants are not received and considered until after the relevant expenditure has been incurred. There is therefore no selectivity as between various industry groups or individual business enterprises, exercised in advance of the IR and D work being performed. Additionally, amendments implemented in 1972 included a further provision requiring applicant companies to undertake in writing that they would exploit on normal commercial terms, and for the benefit of the Australian economy, the results of the research and development, relative to which the application is made.

268. The Australian Industrial Research and Development Grants Board, an independent statutory authority, administers the scheme.

269. In December 1973, a number of amendments to the scheme were enacted. A limit on the amount payable to any one company or its wholly-owned subsidiaries, for any one grant year was introduced. Additionally, the scheme was extended to enable consideration of applications from companies, generally smaller concerns, which performed worthwhile research and development under the direction of personnel possessing practical skills and experience, but lacking the formal qualifications previously required. A comprehensive review of the scheme is currently being undertaken with the aim of increasing its overall effectiveness as an incentive for R and D in Australian industry.

270. In 1973-74 some 957 firms applied for grants. This was an increase of about 79% on the number of applicants in the Scheme's first year of operation. Some 24% of these companies were applying for grants for the first time. From the Scheme's inception in 1967 up to June 1974, $ 73 million was distributed. Grants made during the 1973-74 financial year totalled $ 15 million.

271. One criticism that has been made of the Scheme is that grants received by firms are taxable, hence the net incentive to industrial R and D is rather less than the above figures imply.

272. The broad industry groups that have benefited principally under the Schemes are basic metal products, industrial machinery and equipment, electric and electronic apparatus, transport equipment and chemicals.

273. Another programme which the Government has recently introduced is the "Visiting Industrial Experts Grants Scheme", the prime objective of which, is to assist Australian manufacturing enterprises meet the cost of employing overseas industrial experts, whose services will directly contribute to the development of more efficient and competitive secondary industries by introducing modern overseas technical know-how.

274. Emphasis is on assistance to substantially Australian-owned firms, especially small to medium sized enterprises, which are frequently in a less favourable position, than many overseas-owned firms, in acquiring and utilizing industrial technology developed overseas.

275. Grants are paid on the basis of 20% of eligible expenditure, subject to a maximum grant of $ 10,000 per year for up to three years. Grants will only be paid where it can be shown that the visiting expert can bring necessary expertise not reasonably available within Australia. It must also be demonstrated, that satisfactory arrangements have been made for relevant expertise to be passed on, so as to enable the eventual effective maintenance of the manufacturing project under the supervision of a permanent resident of Australia.

276. The Australian Government also offers financial assistance to the Inventors Association of Australia Ltd., in order to help stimulate the flow of private inventions available to industry, as well as to assist private Australian inventors. The initial government grant was made in 1968-69. For 1974-75 a base grant of $ 10,000 has been made available to the Association together with a grant of $ 10,000 on a $ for $ basis, matched by income from other, non-government, sources.

277. In 1974-75 the Government announced a new scheme to assist private inventors. The scheme, which encompasses the grant to the

Inventors Association of Australia Ltd. , is administered by a specially appointed Advisory Committee and includes together with the $ 20,000 grant to the Association, a grant of $ 150,000 which can be made available in grants up to $ 10,000 per individual for the development of inventions: $ 50,000 for the evaluation of inventions; and $ 8,000 for administration costs.

General Aids

278. A number of diverse programmes, including interfirm comparisons, industrial design and industrial standardization, the Government research organisation, (CSIRO), are listed under this category.

279. Since 1966, the Department of Manufacturing Industry has maintained a small full-time staff to promote interfirm comparisons and assist industries to undertake for themselves this management technique for improving efficiency.

280. The technique of interfirm comparison enables each firm in a relatively homogeneous group to compare its performance over a range of indicators with the norms for the group or industry as a whole.

281. The Australian Government supports good design and innovation as an important multi-disciplinary approach to upgrading products and processes in Australian manufacturing industry.

282. The Industrial Design Council of Australia, a non-governmental body, has received grants from the Australian Government since 1962. In the 1974-75 financial year, $ 420,000 was made available by the Australian Government to the Council.

283. The Council has a variety of design promotion programmes, the principal emphasis being on extension services to manufacturers, and in particular, to small firms and firms in decentralized areas.

284. Standardization is another activity which is an important aid to the efficiency, competitiveness and the diffusion of technology in the industrial sector. For these reasons, the Australian Government supports the Standards Association of Australia both financially, and through direct participation in the Association's technical activities. Grants to the Association in 1974-75 from the Australian Government amounted to $ 1,303,000. Standardization is particularly important in the area of foreign trade, as the progressive reduction of tariff barriers has shown that incompatible standards constitute a non-tariff barrier. Australia is participating in GATT discussions directed at drafting a proposed International Code of Conduct on Standards.

285. The Commonwealth Scientific and Industrial Research Organisation (CSIRO) is historically a mission oriented research body. Its initial orientation was towards work relating to primary industries, but since the 1940s it has conducted a substantial amount of research work

of relevance to manufacturing industry. Industry has access to the research carried out by CSIRO, and is encouraged to utilize and exploit its findings. Experience has shown that the technical competence of industry can be readily improved by the application of CSIRO's results.

Diffusion of Technology

286. In 1972 the then Department of Trade and Industry released the results of a study undertaken for the Department by a firm of private consultants to determine the rate of diffusion of selected new technologies into Australian manufacturing industry. The survey took into account industry group size,* local and overseas ownership, labour and capital intensiveness and R and D capacity. The survey led to the following broad conclusions about Australian industry:

- it was quick to learn of new technology through close contacts with other advanced countries;
- it was quick to adopt and diffuse new technology which required little capital investment, although adoption generally occurred later than in the other advanced countries;
- it was considerably slower than industry in most other advanced countries in first-use of technology which required high or medium capital investment - however, once the innovation was adopted, diffusion occurred reasonably rapidly;
- in general, diffusion of technology was retarded by the small market size but assisted at times by overseas visits and importation of overseas machinery;
- initial use of technology in Australia and its subsequent diffusion throughout industry had been delayed by such factors as absence of early local manufacture of equipment necessary for the innovation, lack of research, facilities, inadequate education and training, lack of strong competition, lack of specialization, small effect of government purchasing power, relatively small government incentives to replace plant and machinery, small size operation, and tariff protection supporting older technologies.

Information Services

287. In 1972 the then Office of Secondary Industry published a "Business Services Guide" aimed at assisting manufacturers to gain a more comprehensive picture of the range of services and facilities available to Australian manufacturing industry, from both private enterprise and government sources.

* The industry groups covered by the survey were plywood, ship building, wool textiles, electronic components, quick frozen food, die casting, plastics, powder metallurgy, heavy organic chemicals and machine tools.

288. Although a growing network of ancillary services had developed in Australia, offering expert advice and assistance in a variety of aspects of business administration, it has become evident that there are a number of problems and barriers inhibiting the use of such facilities by the small business sector. A number of measures which have been introduced, or are in the process of introduction, are directed towards rectifying this situation.

Government Purchasing Policies

289. For many years, Australian Government policy, in relation to its own purchasing, has been to decide between tenders on the basis of best value for money. Although the Government does not pay customs duties, in comparing tenders the appropriate duty is nationally added to the price of overseas goods. Local industry therefore gets the full benefit of the normal protective duties. Provision for exception to this general principle of value for money exists for cases where: procurement in Australia would contribute materially to a particular and significant aspect of national development; the local industry is depressed; or overseas goods are quoted at dumped prices. The present Government has continued to follow this broad approach, pending the outcome of a detailed review of Government policy.

290. In December 1972, the Prime Minister announced that Australian Government contracts should be awarded to an Australian-owned company, in cases where Australian and overseas-owned firms submit tenders which meet specifications and are equal in respect of price and availability. Until then, the general practice with equal tenders had been to accept the tenderer who had been the most recent, satisfactory supplier of identical goods.

291. Running parallel with this basic purchasing policy is the "offset" programme - i. e. the programme to encourage Australian industrial participation in overseas procurement.

292. In November 1973, the Government announced that a Committee would review Government Procurement Policy. The Prime Minister, in announcing the appointment of a committee to enquire into Government purchasing, said "The purpose of the Government in deciding on an enquiry is to ensure that consistent with the aim of securing best value for money, the procurement policies of the Australian Government and, when they are using Australian Government funds, the procurement policies of State and Local Governments are in harmony with national policies relating to the structure of industries, industrial efficiency, technological progress, regional development, the economic and social aspects of employment, pollution and product and product standards testing". Government purchasing is quite relevant as a factor in industrial policy but whether or not it is an instrument of industrial policy is an undecided question at this point of time.

293. In its report, the Committee recommended that, in order to upgrade the procurement function to a degree commensurate with its importance to both Government and industry, an Australian Government Purchasing Commission be established as a central purchasing authority, responsible for the co-ordination of policy, and in time, for the purchase of goods and services for all Government departments, with the possible exception of certain specialized functions. The Committee also recommended that, as soon as possible, the proposed Commission should initiate a thorough overhaul of the principles, rules and regulations governing the procurement function.

v) Small Business Programme

294. As outlined in Chapter 2, small businesses comprise a significant sector of the Australian economy, especially in the manufacturing sector, where 93% of manufacturing establishments employ less than 100 persons. The Government has recently established a National Small Business Bureau to develop and implement a national programme of assistance to small business, in both the manufacturing and tertiary sectors. The programme will embrace research and policy work associated with the operation of small businesses, management development (encompassing training and counselling), collection and dissemination of technological and economic information and other appropriate advisory services.

295. Unlike many other developed countries there has been no arm of the Australian Government with any specific responsibility for the small firm sector until the recent establishment of the Bureau. It is not envisaged that small business should be treated as a preferred or privileged section of the business community. Rather the aim is to provide small enterprises as far as practicable with access to a range of expertise and facilities relevant for their efficient operation and viable development, but which would normally be beyond their own individual capacity to provide.

296. The programme will of necessity be developed gradually. Small businesses vary widely in their characteristics and comprise a large and diverse sector of the economy. The problems of communication alone are very great as many do not belong to traditional groups such as Chambers of Commerce, Industry Associations, etc. There is also a paucity of reliable information on this important sector, its place and contribution to the economy and its special problems and needs.

297. The Bureau has a responsibility to ensure that programmes are based on thorough evaluations of the particular needs of small business and do not duplicate existing services but rather meet gaps and deficiencies which already exist in these services.

298. A most important function of the Bureau in the co-ordination of existing facilities and services for small business provided by the

Government and private sectors. Where deficiencies exist in these facilities the Bureau will aim to encourage the extension of services to fill the deficiency either by the bodies already carrying them out or by the Bureau itself working in conjunction with organisations concerned with the relevant aspect.

299. There are no provisions in the Bureau's charter at present which enable it to provide finance for small firms or to guarantee loans. However, the Bureau has commissioned a research project by consultants to determine the finance needs of small firms and the adequacy of existing finance facilities to meet the needs of small firms. There are at present no special Government supported facilities for providing finance for small firms, with the exception of the Commonwealth Development Bank whose charter includes that of providing finance for the establishment or development of industrial undertakings particularly small undertakings.

## VERTICAL POLICIES

300. Vertical industry policies which have been operative in Australia over recent years can be divided into three categories:

i) those associated with or related to the tariff
ii) those associated with import competition but not related to the tariff
iii) domestic supply assurance policies.

301. In 1969-70, over 90% of manufacturing industry (in value added terms) had tariff protection available (although not necessarily in use), 30% of manufacturing industry having available an average effective rate of more than 50%. This compares with less than 5% of manufacturing industry being influenced by non-tariff related vertical policies (see table 5. 3. ).

### i) Tariff Related Policies

302. As has been mentioned earlier the tariff has been the policy instrument used by successive Australian Governments for the encouragement and development of manufacturing industry. Consequently many of the vertical industry policies have been associated with the tariff or related to changes in it. There are two main types of these policies:

a) Policies adopted to ensure that a particular industry is either established or developed in Australia. In these instances policy references are sent to the Industries Assistance Commission or its predecessor the Tariff Board informing the IAC that the Government wished to preserve an industry in some shape or form, and therefore to recommend appropriate methods and levels of protection. Example of this type of policy are motor vehicles, chemicals, and machine tools;

b) Policies introduced to facilitate adjustment by industries to downward movements in the tariff e. g. apparel, footwear, domestic appliances, and consumer electronics.

Details of these policies are set out below.

Motor Vehicles

303. For over 30 years the Australian Government has been involved in planning the development of a domestic motor vehicles industry.

304. In 1945 the Government invited likely motor vehicle manufacturers to submit plans for the manufacture of motor vehicle chassis. General Motors Holden's proposals for the first Holden were accepted at the end of 1945 and volume production commenced in 1949.

305. The other major overseas companies with assembly operations in Australia, Ford, Leyland and Chrysler also subsequently commenced local manufacture of passenger vehicles. Japanese and European companies have entered into assembly operations either on their own account or through arrangements with assembly companies.

306. In the late 1950s tariffs were at a level set to encourage local component manufacture but, because of gaps in local manufacturing capacity and other factors, duty free by-laws on components were available. With the removal of import licensing in 1960 motor vehicle builders tended to revert to imported components. The Government decided therefore in the mid-1960s to relate the availability of duty concessions under by-law to commitments to increase local content through a system of Plans.

307. In 1965 the Government introduced Plan A, which required manufacturers to achieve 95% local content within five years in return for duty free admission of all residual components. Two low local content Plans with restrictive by-laws were also introduced.

308. The Plans were amended four times between 1966 and 1971:

- in February 1966 by the introduction of low content Assembly Plans following consideration of a Tariff Board report;
- in November 1966 and again in December 1968 (when an 85% Plan was introduced) because of problems in the development of light car manufacture in Australia; and
- in 1971 when a decision was made to phase out the Assembly Plans to overcome problems of fragmentation in the light car market and ensure continued development of high content manufacturing, especially in the light car field.

309. A summary of the local content plans prior to recent policy changes is as follows:

| | LOCAL CONTENT | VOLUME LIMITS | BY-LAW DUTY FREE CONCESSIONS |
|---|---|---|---|
| Manufacturing Plans | 95%<br>85% | No limit<br>25,000 p. a. | (all residual components) |
| Assembly Plans | 60%<br>50%<br>45% | 7,500 p. a.<br>5,000 p. a.<br>2,500 p. a. | 20% in 1972<br>15% in 1973<br>10% in 1974<br>nil from 1. 1. 1975 |

310. In August 1973 the Australian Government laid down new rules and objectives for the Australian motor vehicle industry and referred the question of assistance for passenger motor vehicles and components to the IAC. The IAC (then the Tariff Board) was asked to advise on how best to achieve the Government's objectives.

311. The objectives were to improve the efficiency with which the community's productive resources are used, to recognize the interests of consumers, and to create an industry operating at the highest possible level of efficiency and economic management with high Australian content. The vehicles must afford a high level of safety in construction and use, and have effective antipollution devices. The industry must be well located for social, employment and environmental purposes. There should be improved labour relations and production techniques, and substantial Australian participation, including equity, in the industry.

312. The IAC presented its report on the passenger motor vehicle industry to the Government in mid-July 1974. In its report, the IAC recommended immediate abandonment of the local content plans, and a long-term rate of 25% on both vehicles and components. However, to minimize disruption, an interim rate of 35% was proposed until 1980, then 30% until 1982. Duties at that time were 34% on vehicles and 26% on most components.

313. The Government's consideration of the IAC Report which extended over a period of three months included detailed discussions with all interested parties. As a result of these discussions a number of alternative proposals were formulated which were considered together with the IAC Report.

314. The Prime Minister announced on 14th November, 1974 new measures to assist and strengthen the Australian motor vehicle industry. Further details of the plan were announced in mid-December. Some aspects remain for further decision.

315. The Government accepted the judgement of the Industries Assistance Commission that the Australian motor industry should be

restructured and has moved to correct some inadequacies associated with past protection policies by reducing the multiplicity of motor vehicle plans to a single 85% local content plan and changing the basic plan from a model to a company basis. There will be a four year phase-in period. By-law concessions under the plan will encourage regional complementation arrangements.

316. The plan, which is to operate for ten years, will be supported by a tariff of 35% on completely built up (CBU) imports and 25% on completely knocked down (CKD) imports. However, when imports exceed 20% of total new passenger motor vehicle registrations these tariffs are to increase by 10% points to 45% and 35% respectively. In view of the abnormal levels of imports during the latter part of 1974, the higher duties were effective immediately.

317. On 20th December the Government decided that, consistent with its desire that change in the industry should be manageable, the increased duty rate on CKD assembly packs and major components for the original equipment market would be phased-in over a four year period on the following basis (i. e. , if imports remain above the 20% level).

| JAN. 1975 | 1.1.76 | 1.1.77 | 1.1.78 | 1.1.79 |
|---|---|---|---|---|
| 27½% | 30% | 32½% | 32½% | 35% |

If during the phasing period the duty on CBU's should fall from 45% to 35%, the rate on CKD packs will return to 25%.

318. Imports of components for the replacement market are to be dutiable at 25%.

319. It is envisaged that these new long-term policy measures will allow the industry to more readily exploit the advantages of economies of scale, component commonality and regional complementation. The new measures will develop a stronger long-term base for the local industry and at the same time allow the industry to adjust more easily to basic structural changes essential for its future growth and viability.

320. As from 1st February, 1975 quantitative restrictions were applied to imports of passenger and light commercial vehicles. The effect of the controls will be to limit imports during 1975 of new and second-hand assembled passenger cars to 90,000 units. Controls on assembled light commercial vehicles (i. e. up to 2,722 kg) will ensure that imports do not, in 1975, exceed the level attained in 1974. The restrictions are being applied as a temporary measure to prevent damage to the Australian motor vehicle manufacturing industry which would be difficult to repair.

321. During 1974 imports of completely assembled new passenger motor vehicles totalled 151,042 compared with 65,697 in the previous year. Over the last three months of 1974 the rate of imports accelerated sharply to 16,719 units a month as against an average of 5,740 a month over the same period of 1973. The increase in imports was in excess of market growth, resulting in a heavy build-up of unsold stocks of which about 60,000 were the output of Australian producers. Employment in Australian motor vehicle manufacturing had already been reduced and further large-scale retrenchments would have taken place unless there was a substantial reduction in stocks of unsold vehicles.

322. Simultaneously with the introduction of the measures outlined above, the Australian Government took fiscal measures to stimulate demand within Australia for motor vehicles. These measures, which apply to vehicles both domestically produced and imported, include a temporary reduction in sales tax and the repeal of a recently introduced income tax provision which had the effect of dampening demand by fleet owners.

Chemicals

323. The manufacture of chemicals began in Australia in the 1920s but it was not until after World War II that rapid growth occurred. The long-term development of the industry has been stimulated by the post-war development of many new industries such as plastics, detergents and nitrogenous fertilizers.

324. The industry includes two major complexes, one based in Sydney, NSW and one in Atona, Victoria. The Australian industry is small by world standards due mainly to the relatively small size of the domestic market.

325. The disability of a small domestic market together with some degree of surplus plant capacity accentuated by plant duplication and fragmentation as well as the development of large scale, low cost overseas plants created problems for the chemical industry in Australia during the early 1960s.

326. In October 1963, the Government responded to representations by the industry and referred the whole chemical industry to the Australian Tariff Board for inquiry and report.

327. The reference indicated a desire on the part of the Government to achieve a reasonably profitable development of a soundly based chemical industry, maximum economic development and utilization of various products of the industry as a whole, effective protection from competition from imports at dumped or disruptively low prices and effective and stable protection of employment and investment in the chemical and closely related industries (e.g. plastics industry).

328. In the Tariff Board's subsequent report on the industry, the Board recommended industry tariff rates of 25% ad valorem for simple processes and 40% ad valorem for capital intensive petro-chemical production.

329. In addition special rates above 40% and support values were also introduced. "Support values" are a non-tariff system intended to counter disruptively priced imports. The support value duty is equal to 67.5% of the difference between the support value and the landed cost, the latter being the sum of the f.o.b. price, freight and insurance and customs duty. The difference is known as the support value differential. The calculation of support values is based on representative duty paid costs of the particular chemical when f.o.b. prices are free of dumping and other elements of price disruption, and when shipping freight and other costs are in accordance with those generally charged for the type of goods concerned. The system of support value duties currently applies to less than 1% of the items in the Tariff.

330. The revenue, if any, from this system is not used for any specific purpose, it goes simply to revenue and it is not possible to estimate the amount charged each year because it relates to world prices. If suddenly there is disruptive pricing the support value applies, if not - it does not.

331. A programme of regular reviews of the assistance accorded to the Australian chemical industry was also recommended by the Tariff Board.

332. The Government accepted the Board's recommendations and in 1968 and 1971 further reports were presented by the Tariff Board resulting in changes in the levels of some support values with new support values added and some removed. The industry is scheduled to be reviewed again by the IAC towards the end of 1975.

Metal Working Machine Tools

333. In 1968 the Government referred to the Tariff Board the question of assistance to the metal working machine tools industry following representations by the local industry. The industry claimed that because of the small local market and irregular demand, they were unable to take advantage of economies of scale to reduce costs and thus compete successfuly with imports. The reference requested the Tariff Board to have regard to the Government's objective that at least the nucleus of a machine tools industry should be maintained in Australia and also to take account of the Government's desire that the machine tools industry should not be encouraged to expand beyond the range within which it was then operating.

334. In response to the Government's reference, the Tariff Board in April 1972 recommended that:

- certain power fed machines should in addition to tariff assistance receive assistance by bounty;
- certain special purpose machines subject to minimum rates of duty should receive assistance by bounty;
- the majority of the remaining machines under reference should continue to receive tariff assistance at rates of 35% General, 25% Preferential. These rates are now 26% and 19% respectively following the 25% across the board tariff reduction in July 1973.

335. The bounty is payable at 33 1/3 % of the ex-factory selling price of the machine, reduced by 1% for each 1% by Australia content falls below 85%. The bounty is not payable if the Australian content of ex-factory cost is below 55% and is payable only in respect of machines manufactured on premises registered under the Metal Working Machine Tools Bounty Act 1972.

Apparel

336. Present levels of assistance to the apparel industry in general reflect the high levels of duties imposed during the 1930s which were intended to encourage employment creating activities within Australia. The levels of assistance are currently being reviewed by the Industries Assistance Commission. The report is expected in 1976.

337. Competition from low cost imports in a small section of the apparel industry (shirts and some knitted outerwear) led to an inquiry by the Tariff Board which, in 1971, recommended a lowering of duties on the goods concerned. Because these sectors of the apparel industry involved significant employment, the Government took steps to provide the industry with time to restructure its activities. The Government endeavoured to enter voluntary restraint arrangements with the three main supplying developing countries. When these negotiations were unsuccessful, the quantitative restrictions which had been imposed temporarily were replaced by tariff quotas which were removed at the end of February 1974.

338. As part of its procedures for action under the GATT Textiles Arrangements, the Government has appointed a Textiles Authority within the Industries Assistance Commission to inquire and report on references, asking whether action should be taken under the Arrangement. The Authority is required to report within 60 days.

339. Australia recently experienced a substantial growth in imports of textile and apparel goods resulting from, among other things, revaluation policies, the 25% tariff cut and the removal of tariff quotas on certain apparel items. Imports of fibres, yarns and fabrics were 70% higher in the year to June 1974 than the year earlier. Imports of apparel goods, virtually all competitive with Australian production,

increased by 94% over the same period. Employment in larger private factories fell by 16% between March and September 1974 and significant retrenchments occurred in the small businesses. As the textile industry is a major employer of female labour - it is also the major employer in a number of country towns - the retrenchment caused considerable structural unemployment.

340. Because of the disruptive effect of import competition on many segments of the industry and the development of consequential social problems of some magnitude, the Government took a series of actions, generally, based on the findings of the Textiles Authority. The Government took action to stabilize the situation either by initiating voluntary restraint arrangements in terms of the GATT Textiles Arrangement, where such action would effectively remove the market disruption or by the introduction of a system of tariff quotas, in accordance with Australia's rights under the GATT, where this was appropriate or necessary.

341. This action on some textile and apparel products is considered to be of a short-term nature. It is intended that the action taken establishes an appropriate balance between imports and local production to ensure that employment opportunities are not disrupted; to slow down the fast and disruptive rate of change that is taking place; and to subsequently achieve a relatively stable situation so that rationalization and restructuring can be induced at an acceptable rate.

Footwear

342. All told the Tariff Board has reported on the Australian footwear industry on eleven occasions with the last two reports in 1966 and 1970 covering the whole industry and non-leather uppers segment respectively.

343. In its 1966 report the Board recommended industry rates of 45% General and 25% Preferential or alternative specific rates which were intended to protect the industry against low priced disruptive competition. The Board commented that these rates should provide adequate long-term protection for efficient local manufacturers whilst also providing a sound basis for the industry to continue its reorganisation.

344. The alternative specific duties were recommended to offer some extra assistance to two categories of manufacturers:

a) those which through not incurring significant cost disadvantages on raw materials, required extra protection for a limited period to assist them to achieve more competitive forms of production; and

b) those which incurred substantial disadvantages by using certain costly local raw materials.

345. The Government accepted the Board's recommendations including the request that the product categories to which the specific rates applied be referred to the Board in about three years time.

346. The 1970 report observed that the readjustment and rationalization of the Australian footwear industry had continued with the more viable sections of the industry increasing their sales and profitability. The Board considered that the industry should not require assistance additional to the industry rates of 45% General and 25% Preferential and therefore recommended that the alternative specific rates be phased out over a period of five years. The phase-down period was recommended as the Board felt that local producers should be further assisted to readjust to the changing circumstances of the industry and its market. The Government accepted the Board's recommendation.

347. In 1974 a situation similar to that in textiles also occurred in footwear. The increase in imports has been so large and so sudden that the economy has not been able to absorb the impact. As an indication of the disruption caused, 203 firms in the textiles, clothing and footwear industries have approached the Department of Manufacturing Industry concerning assistance under the Adjustment Assistance Programme. Imports of all types of footwear increased from 17 million pairs in 1972-73 to over 29 million pairs in 1973-74, an increase of 70%. The imports of leather footwear, Australia's most competitive segment of the industry, rose by over 80%. Prior to 1973-74, these imports were relatively stable. At the end of 1973-74 imports commanded 40% of the Australian market, compared with 29% at the end of 1972-73, and 27% at the end of 1971-72. As a result of this large increase in imports which carried on into the first three months of 1974-75, the Prime Minister referred the industry to the Temporary Assistance Authority in September 1974. The Government accepted, in principle, the Temporary Assistance Authority's Report which involved a public enquiry and imposed temporary import restrictions on most types of footwear from 18th October, 1974. The import restrictions are intended to limit imports over the next twelve months to a level 20% higher than the level of imports in 1972-73 for each specified product with provision for increased quotas in the next twelve months. Imports over the next twelve months would, therefore, be about 30% less in 1973-74.

## Domestic Appliances

348. In recent years the Australian market for domestic appliances has been supplied mainly by local manufacturers. Levels of tariff protection were generally high and although some rationalization had occurred the industry was characterized by a large number of production units manufacturing a wide variety of products and models in a relatively small domestic market; these features contributed towards cost disabilities compared with overseas suppliers.

349. As part of the general tariff review programme, the domestic appliance industry was referred to the Tariff Board and on 23rd January, 1974 the Government announced its decision on the recommendations

in the Board's report. Products covered by the report and decision included refrigerators, washing machines, air conditioners, cooking equipment and portable appliances (toasters, irons, mixers, vacuum cleaners, fans, etc. ).

350. Generally the Government accepted, with minor variations, the Board's recommendations, which provided for the then existing tariff rates for a number of goods to be reduced significantly. Compared with the rates prevailing before the across the board tariff cut of one-quarter in July 1973, the reductions were even more marked. In place of the previous multiplicity of rates, a tariff of 25% was approved for most of the goods with the few exceptions carrying rates within the 20% to 35% range.

351. The recommended duties on some of the goods took effect on 4th February, 1974. However, reduced duties on the other goods, for which the Board had recommended a two year deferral of the tariff changes, are now subject to a phased implementation over two years. This planning was designed to provide firms with a more gradual increase in competitive pressures and encourage them to start undertaking the necessary re-organisation at an early date with the object of spreading the impact on production and employment patterns.

352. In broadly accepting the Board's recommendations the Government was mindful of the Board's view that there were indications that major economies could be achieved in the industry through the re-organisation of production activities. Such economies would allow the industry sectors involved to operate profitably and probably command a larger market under reduced levels of protection. Duty levels were therefore set at levels designed to encourage a better use of resources while providing adequate protection for the more efficient producers. It was considered that the better use of resources and the lower levels of tariff protection should bring significantly reduced prices to consumers (than would otherwise have prevailed) as well as general economic benefits to the community as a whole.

353. One of the items covered by the Government's decision was given special treatment. A bounty is to be paid for two years on the production and sale in Australia of certain sealed unit refrigeration compressors because of the importance of these compressors as components in the manufacture of refrigerators and room air conditioners. The bounty provides local refrigerator and air conditioner manufacturers with the immediate advantage of lower costs in relation to an important component and thereby assist them to prepare for the reduced level of protection on their appliances. At the same time the bounty allows the local compressor industry time to adapt to the immediate reduction in its tariff protection.

354. Overall the Government's policy towards the domestic appliance industry is aimed at bringing about significant changes in some sectors

of the industry as part of its broad policy of encouraging increased industrial efficiency. In recognition of the possible impact of the tariff changes on domestic appliances, the Government decided in principle that assistance would be made available to firms and employees disadvantaged by the changes. Such assistance was to be in accordance with the general adjustment assistance principles which were then under consideration by the Government.

355. During the fiscal year 1973-74 imports of refrigerators (200-454 litres), clothes dryers and clothes washing machines increased by 194%, 143% and 45% respectively. In the light of the preceding, the Prime Minister referred the industry to the Temporary Assistance Authority. Following consideration of the recommendations of the Authority, the Government has decided to introduce, as from 1st March, 1975 and for the duration of one year, tariff quotas on domestic electrical refrigerators of 200 litres or above and electric-mechanical clothes drying machines and clothes washing machines.

Electronics Industry

356. In december 1972, the question of the level of protection afforded to the production of the electronics industry in Australia was referred to the Tariff Board for inquiry and report.

357. Up to that time the level of tariff protection applicable to these goods varied considerably but was characterized by quite high specific rates of duty on many components and consumer products. When it reported to the Government on 27th September, 1973 on Consumer Electronic Equipment and Components, the Tariff Board stated that "existing duties, in ad valorem terms, range from nil to over 1,000%".

358. On 19th November, 1973, the Prime Minister announced that consumer electronic equipment and most electronic components would be dutiable at 35% on and from 20th November, 1973. The Prime Minister said that Government accepted the basic thrust of the above report. This, he said, would provide the Australian consumer with a wider range of cheaper electronic consumer goods, including colour television receivers.

359. He also announced that the Government has approved in principle the introduction of subsidy assistance on selected electronic components because of their technological, telecommunication or defence significance, with such assistance being available at least until the later report on professional electronic equipment was considered by the Government.

360. Following consideration of reports by various consultants commissioned by the Government and information supplied by the Departments of Defence, Science, Postmaster-General, Transport and Manufacturing Industry and the CSIRO, the Minister for Manufacturing Industry announced on 8th July, 1974, that the Government had

agreed that production of selected electronic components should be maintained in Australia at least until the Industries Assistance Commission reports on the professional sectors of the electronics industry are considered by the Government.

361. The nominated components are: integrated and thick film circuits; special purpose transducers; printed circuit boards; and certain types of: discrete semiconductors; quartz crystals; resistors capacitors; vacuum tubes; transformers and inductors.

362. After consideration of the information currently available to it, the Government believed production of these components (with the exception of transmitting valves) would continue in Australia in the short-term without further assistance by the Government. However, any change in these circumstances will be quickly considered by the Government.

363. In the case of transmitting valves, the Government had decided to grant immediate subsidy assistance for their production to ensure supply of valves to Government users. The Government later also decided to provide a subsidy to a company manufacturing integrated circuits and semi-conductors. Other cases are under consideration.

364. The Government has therefore made it quite clear that it would like to see Australian production of these nominated components continued at least until the Professional Electronic Equipment report is considered.

365. These substantial changes in tariff protection afforded to the Australian Electronics industry will no doubt cause some restructuring in the industry. It is too early to outline what the long-term structure of the electronics industry might be. However, the production of small transistor radios has already ceased. Local manufacture of small monochrome television receivers is also declining as import pressures build up, while component manufacturers are generally looking to phasing out production of some items for use in consumer electronic equipment.

366. In early 1975 the Government forwarded a reference to the Temporary Assistance Authority covering a wide range of consumer electronic equipment and components. The Authority's report recommended that temporary assistance by means of an additional duty of 10% be given to the production of: monochrome television receivers and picture tubes with a screen size of not less than seventeen inches (43 cm); certain fixed electrical capacitors; ferrite cores; slugs and other shapes; and loud-speakers. Additional protection was not found to be necessary at that time for the other goods under reference, which included colour television receivers and audio equipment. The Government accepted the Authority's recommendations in April 1975.

ii) Non-tariff Policies

367. On occasions the Government has found that the tariff is not always the most appropriate form of protection against import competition. For instance the Government may want production of an item in Australia to continue but does not wish the cost of the product to the user industry to be increased by a tariff e. g. ships and products used by the pastoral and agricultural industries such as tractors and fertilizers.

368. The general policy relating to bounties in Australia is that they are accorded in the following circumstances:

- when the output of the protected industry will supply only a small proportion of Australian requirements;
- when the industry using the protected product is an export-oriented industry dependent on world prices; the tractor industry is a case in point, tractor costs being a contributing factor to the overall costs of the export-oriented primary industries;
- when the protected product is the raw material at the base of a chain of operations of further manufacture distribution;
- when the excess cost of an industry that is desirable on other than economic grounds e. g. defence reasons, is so high that use of the product would be discouraged.

369. Normally bounties involve a profit limitation clause, usually around 10% on funds employed. Bounties are accorded for definite time periods such as a given number of years, and if they are not allowed to expire, they are subject to review. The IAC Act, for example, provides that where financial assistance to an industry has been provided for a period of not less than six years, the Commission on its own initiative may enquire into and report on that assistance.

370. Another instance where tariff protection is inappropriate is for goods listed in Annex A to United Nations Agreement on the Importation of Educational Scientific and Cultural Materials. An instance of this is the policy pertaining to the Book Manufacturing Industry.

Shipbuilding Industry

371. In recent years the Australian shipbuilding industry has been assisted by a subsidy rather than a tariff, so as to avoid adding to the operating costs of shipping operators. The subsidy scheme has been supported by an import prohibition which prevented ships being imported except with the approval of the Minister for Transport.

372. The Government's current policy is to provide assistance to the shipbuilding industry in a form and at a level which will assure the continuing development of a rationalized shipbuilding industry in Australia. This assistance is to be closely aligned with assistance

accorded to manufacturing industry generally, and is intended to sustain economic production and alleviate local shipbuilders' disabilities against prospective import competition while providing the opportunity for intending purchasers to source their requirements overseas.

373. On 18th December, 1973 the Government announced details of new arrangements to assist shipbuilding in Australia. Previously, import controls had ensured that virtually all continuing domestic requirements for vessels over 200 tons gross were supplied by local shipbuilders and a generous subsidy of up to 45% of construction cost was paid on vessels built in Australia for use in Australian waters. Taken together these measures provided protection of a very high order and involved total subsidy payments of $ 30.7 million in 1972-73 compared with $ 13.4 million in 1971-72.

374. The Government considered these forms of assistance were exceptional by comparison with other areas of manufacturing industry, and accordingly sought to provide assistance which would meet the policy objectives outlined above.

375. Briefly, the new assistance arrangements are as follows:

Level of subsidy

The level of subsidy is to be phased down from its present maximum level of 45% to a maximum of 25% by 31st December, 1980. The maximum level is determined by a formula whereby a subsidy of 25% is paid on vessels up to 1,000 tons gross, increasing by $2\frac{1}{2}$% points of each 1,000 tons gross or part thereof until the maximum level in accordance with the phase-down is reached.

Vessels exceeding 90,000 deadweight tons and offshore oil drilling vessels for use in Australian waters are eligible for subsidy at the rate of 25%.

Vessels eligible for subsidy

Subsidy is payable in respect of vessels exceeding 150 tons gross and fishing vessels 21 metres or more in length. Subsidy is not payable on exports, with the exception of vessels for use in international trade by Australian flag operators. There is provision of recapture of subsidy on a pro-rata basis is a vessel built under subsidy is, within 10 years, disposed of for use outside Australian waters by other than Australian flag operators.

Import controls

New vessels remain subject to import controls, but approval to import will be given if the after-subsidy price of the lowest acceptable Australian tender is higher than the overseas tender price including delivery (compared on a cash payment basis).

The arrangements require that Australian shipyards be given a reasonable opportunity to submit tenders, and the price of the overseas tender is an undumped price.

Credit facilities

The Government is currently considering whether it will make available long-term credit facilities at moderate interest rates to shipbuilders and, if so, the way in which such facilities will be provided.

Registration of shipyards

Subsidy is payable only to shipyards registered with the Government for the purposes of the scheme. Shipyards engaged in ship construction as at 18th December, 1973 are eligible for registration in respect of the sizes and types of vessels which they had previously constructed. Requests for registration from interests who had not (as at 18th December, 1973) previously engaged in shipbuilding activity or from current shipyards in respect of vessels outside agreed ranges would be approved where the Government is satisfied that extension of subsidy assistance would contribute towards the orderly development of the industry.

## Agricultural Tractors

376. The Tariff Board reported on the level of assistance for local production of agricultural wheeled tractors in December 1966 recommending assistance by means of a combination of bounty on local production and duties on imports. The Government accepted the Board's recommendation in respect of bounty payments but dit not implement the recommendation for duties on imported tractors. When referring these assistance arrangements back to the Board for further review in October 1970 the Government directed the Board to have regard in the framing of its recommendations "to the Government's desire that users of tractors should have access to tractors at prices which are not increased by any protective measures". The Board reported on this reference in December 1972 recommending assistance by bounty alone. The scale of bounty payments recommended by the Board was accepted by the Government and the Board's report is the basis of the current assistance arrangements.

377. The main features of the current bounty arrangements as set out in the Agricultural Tractors Bounty Act 1966-73 are as follows:

- bounty is restricted to agricultural wheeled tractors, and derivatives thereof, manufactured at premises registered under the Act and sold for use in Australia or an external Territory of Australia (i. e. exports are not eligible for bounty);

- the level of bounty payable varies according to the power rating of the tractor at the power take-off rising from $ 1,040 (at 15 kw at the power take-off) to $ 1,560 (at 67 kw at the power take-off); and
- the level of bounty is also related to the level of Australian content, the amount of bounty payable being reduced by 1½% for each 1% by which the Australian content is less than 90%. Where the Australian content is less than 55% no bounty is payable.

378. These assistance arrangements will be again reviewed by the Industries Assistance Commission prior to the expiry of the present Act on 31st December, 1976.

379. Total bounty payments over recent years have been as follows:

| | |
|---|---|
| 1970-71 | $ 2.7 m. |
| 1971-72 | $ 3.2 m. |
| 1972-73 | $ 2.8 m. |
| 1973-74 | $ 3.7 m. |

Printing and Publishing Industries

380. The policy of successive Australian Governments has been not to impede by tariffs or quota restrictions the importation into Australia of goods listed in Annex A to the United Nations Agreement on the Importation of Educational, Scientific and Cultural Materials, which are admissible into Australia free of customs duty.

381. In keeping with this policy and to maintain an Australian book manufacturing industry which was facing severe competition from imports the Australian Government on 1st June, 1969 introduced a book bounty, payable at a rate of 25% of the total cost of production of each eligible book.

382. The bounty was introduced as an interim measure of assistance pending the outcome of an inquiry by the former Tariff Board (now the Industries Assistance Commission) into products of the printing industry. As a result of the Board's findings the Government recently has agreed to the bounty being increased to 33 1/3 % of the net ex-factory price to the publisher or, if the manufacturer is also the publisher, 33 1/3% of the cost of production. The new rate is to apply to books produced between 18th December, 1973 and 31st December, 1978. The Commission will again review the bounty before 31st December, 1978.

383. Following the introduction of the bounty measures in 1969 the Government established an advisory body, the Book Manufacturing Advisory Panel, comprising representatives of publishers, manufacturers

and Government departments, to maintain a constant review of the situation. This body will continue to function at least until the proposed review of the bounty scheme in 1978.

iii) Domestic Supply Assurance Policies

384. One type of government policy introduced in recent years and which may become increasingly common in years to come is the establishment of an industry panel representing all levels of industry to assess supply levels and advise Government on possible action to ensure adequate domestic supply availability. Although Australia has a number of operative industry panels which are discussed in the next chapter, there are currently only two "supply" panels namely the Oilseeds, Vegetable Oils and Allied Products Panel, and the Copper Panel.

385. The Australian Government established an industry/Government Panel to advise it on the supply of and demand for these products in Australia following the decision by the United States and Canada in July 1973 to place an export embargo on oilseeds, fats and oils and allied products. In addition to Government representatives, growers, processors and user industries were represented on the Panel. Although the export embargoes imposed by the United States and Canada have since been removed following an easing in the world supply situation the Panel has continued to operate.

386. To assist the Panel in its deliberations, quarterly assessments of developments in these and associated industries are provided. The assessments include:

- information on current and future crop prospects in Australia, obtained both from official data and from assessments by grower representatives;
- resumes of international developments in the oilseeds industries and related areas (such as fishmeal production) which are likely to affect the local situation; and
- quarterly details of the supply/demand situation in Australia compiled from information supplied by processors, user industries, importers and exporters.

387. Establishment of the Panel has brought all sectors of the industry together in an endeavour to provide expert advice to the Government, thereby providing the basis upon which future decisions affecting the industry can be made. Conversely, the Panel provides a channel through the industry representatives for disseminating information to all firms and individuals who are participating in the industry.

388. Another major policy instrument which can be but is rarely used by the Government to assure domestic supplies is export control. Products which are subject to export control, that is, Government

permission must be sought before the product can be exported, are listed in the Customs (Prohibited Exports) Regulations. It is very rare for permission not to be forthcoming.

389. An example of one case where controls did operate was in April 1974 when the Government introduced controls on the export of copper from Australia. The need for this control arose from a lack of adequate supplies being available to Australian manufacturers at the pegged Australian copper price. The international copper price at the time was at record levels. By maintaining sufficient supplies of copper for Australian industry at the pegged price, the Government was able to ensure the continued economic operation of these manufactures albeit at the cost of foregone export revenue from the sale overseas of copper ore and copper scrap.

# VI

## INSTITUTIONAL FRAMEWORK

390. As already explained Australia's industrial policy should be viewed as not being separate in itself but as being complementary to and closely interrelated with the Government's overall economic policy. Although there is a separate Cabinet Minister responsible for manufacturing industry, the areas of responsibility of a number of other Ministers also impinge on manufacturing industry policy. Naturally these interrelationships flow through to the departmental level (see Table 6. 1).

391. In December 1972, the Government created a separate Department of Secondary Industry (recently renamed the Department of Manufacturing Industry) out of the then Department of Trade and Industry and a separate Minister was allocated this portfolio in the Federal Cabinet. The role of the new Department was to advise the Government on policies designed to encourage and promote the development and efficiency of Australian secondary industry within the context of economic and related policies. The structure of the Department is outlined in Table 6. 2.

392. Other departments, whose role has a bearing on the formulation of an overall industry policy include; the Department of the Special Minister of State where the Protection Policy Division deals with the co-ordination of advice on protection policy including tariff and other forms of selective assistance to industries; the Department of the Prime Minister and Cabinet where the Projects Division deals with the co-ordination of advice on prices and related matters including the Prices Justification Tribunal; the Department of Overseas Trade which is responsible for the maintenance and development of Australia's international trading position, the negotiation of commodity commitments and agreements, the development of export markets and formulation of policy proposals for the Government on Australia's trade policy and policy objectives; the Department of Urban and Regional Development which deals with matters relating to city and regional planning and development including assistance to and co-operation with the States and local Governments; the Department of Minerals and Energy which deals with evaluation and balanced development of mineral and energy resources; having regard to future requirements, and the Department of Labour which deals with manpower policy proposals, effective placement of labour, investigation of labour supply and demand and general labour policies.

393. In many instances therefore it is necessary for consultations to take place between several departments before a policy proposal is submitted through a Minister to the Cabinet for discussion. The usual vehicle used by departments for such consultations is an Interdepartmental Committee (IDC).

394. In most cases the Interdepartmental Committee is of an ad hoc nature being specially established for a particular purpose. However when a particular matter is likely to continue for some time a Standing IDC is established. One of the most important Standing IDC's is the Standing Interdepartmental Committee on Assistance to Industries (SIDCAI). It was formed in April 1973 to co-ordinate at the departmental level questions of assistance to industry. An important part of the Committee's co-ordination function is concerned with servicing the Government's relationship with the Industries Assistance Commission. In essence the Committee:

1) provides the point for consultation by departments prior to the development of policy advice to Ministers;
2) ensures that all relevant factors are taken into account during the consideration of Industries Assistance Commission reports and the preparation of policy advice to Ministers: and
3) generally facilitates the co-ordination of views and action at the departmental level.

In addition, since the introduction of structural adjustment measures the Committee has been given the functions of:

a) advising whether particular structural changes justify the application of structural adjustment measures; and
b) advising on modifications or extensions of structured adjustment measures.

395. SIDCAI is composed of representatives of the Department of the Special Minister of State (which provides the Chairman of the Committee), the Treasury and the Industry department or departments relevant to the particular matters under consideration (e. g. the Department of Manufacturing Industry when assistance to that sector is being considered). It is the responsibility of departments to consult the Committee on matters having relevance to its responsibilities.

396. The Committee is responsible for advising the Special Minister of State on his submissions to Cabinet relating to IAC reports, and is to be consulted in all cases before proposals for tariff or other selective forms of assistance to industry are put to the Economic Committee of Cabinet or the full Cabinet.

Trade Unions and employer organisations

397. A feature of industrial relations in Australia is that both workers and employers are highly organised into associations. On the union

side there are about $2\frac{1}{2}$ million trade union members, representing some 53% of the Australian work force. There are 294 trade unions, a number which is declining slowly through amalgamations, and most of them are affiliated with State or national bodies. Similarly, employers are organised into both national and industry organisations, but precise figures of membership are not available.

Trade Union Organisations

398. There are four national trade unions federations in Australia. The largest, which comprises mostly "blue collar" unions, is the Australian Council of Trade Unions (ACTU), which came into being in 1927, and in 1973 covered 124 affiliated unions with a total membership of 1.7 million. The Australian Council of Salaried and Professional Associations (ACSPA), was established in 1956, and has 31 affiliated unions with a total membership of about 350,000 drawn largely from the fields of banking, insurance, local government, nursing, teaching, science and technology. The Council of Professional Associations (CPA), covering professional as distinct from clerical workers, was also formed in 1956. It comprises a number of professional associations in the Australian Public Service, together with the Association of Professional Engineers, and has a membership of about 20,000. Finally, the Council of Commonwealth Public Service Organisations (CCPSO), which was formed in 1922, is confined to the Australian Public Service and its affiliated associations, which have a combined membership of about 100,000. Another body known as the Australian Public Service Federation represents associations of employees in the Public Services of the various States.

399. In recent years moves have taken place to effect an amalgamation of some other form of association between the various trade union federations but no formal arrangements exist at this stage. However, on many issues there is close liaison between the ACTU, ACSPA and CCPSO.

Employer Associations

400. As with trade unions, there is no single national employers' federation. Basically, employer associations developed late in the last century in order to balance the growth of the trade union movement in the individual colonies or States. With federation in 1900, State or local employer groups began to form national organisations. However, even today the State employer bodies are generally more direct participants in industrial relations than are national bodies.

401. Basically, employer associations fall into two types; the first, those of a broad character covering a variety of industries or enterprises, and the second, those concerned primarily with particular industries. In the first category are the Chambers of Manufacturers

and the Employers' Federations; in the latter category are organisations such as the Metal Trades Industry Association and the Master Builders' Associations.

402. The two major general organisations at the national level are the Australian Council of Employers' Federations (ACEF) and the Associated Chambers of Manufactures of Australia (ACMA). The two major organisations in the second category which have a voice at the top levels of employers' policy making are the Metal Trades Industry Association (MTIA) and the Australian Wool Growers and Graziers' Council (AWGC).

403. Apart from the general associations covering a wide range of industries and enterprises, strong employer associations exis on an industry basis in significant areas; for example metal trades, stevedoring, shipping, building, vehicle manufacture, retailing, oil and banking. These associations may have affiliations with the other major associations but within the particular industry are dominant in their own right. The MTIA spans the whole range of metal trades, a most significant area in Australian industrial relations, to the extent that it has become an important and influential organisation, virtually similar to the two major general organisations at national level.

404. In recent years, to match the great importance of the ACTU as the national trade union body, the employers have endeavoured to bring their national bodies closer together. They have established what is known as the National Employers' Association (NEA), which is comprised of some 34 National Employer Associations which have come together in a loose semi-formal body to determine employer policy in industrial matters of national importance. Two single companies - BHP and Qantas - are also members of the NEA.

405. In 1961, the NEA formally adopted a procedure for the determination of policy on major issues. To achieve proper co-operation for national industrial proceedings it resolved that:

- it would meet at least twice each year to consider general policy matters;
- a National Employers' Policy Committee (NEPC) be formed and be responsible to the NEA for general supervision of the conduct of national industrial proceedings;
- a National Employers' Industrial Committee be formed to undertake research, subject to direction from the Policy Committee, and supervise the detailed conduct of national industrial proceedings.

406. The National Employers' Policy Committee is generally recognized as the employers' equivalent to the ACTU. It is accepted as principal spokesman in major matters before the Conciliation and Arbitration Commission and has been prominent in national wage,

annual leave and other major matters coming before the Commission. It also represents employer interests in any tripartite discussions between the Australian Government and the trade union movement.

407. A new body to co-ordinate the activities of the two truly national employer bodies, i. e. ACMA and ACEF was formed in 1972. This is the Central Industrial Secretariat. Its membership comprises the Australian Council of Employers' Federations, the Associated Chambers of Manufactures of Australia, all State Employers' Federations and all State Chambers of Manufactures. It comprises a Central Council and a Secretariat. The two national bodies each have two representatives on the controlling council and each State body has one.

408. The Central Industrial Secretariat can be seen as the initial step towards a total merger between ACMA and ACEF on a national level and between the Employers' Federations and Chambers of Manufactures in each State. Such a merger has already taken place in Western Australia and Tasmania and detailed negotiations are at present under way in other States and at the national level.

409. Although the functions of the National Employers' Policy Committee and the Central Industrial Secretariat are similar i. e. formulation of national policy, the two bodies operate in different areas with the CIS on a manpower membership base. However, because of the strength of the organisations comprising the Central Industrial Secretariat in the NEPC it is difficult to envisage a situation in which CIS national policy would diverge substantially from that of the NEPC.

## GOVERNMENT - INDUSTRY DIALOGUE

### Government - Industry Panels

410. In early 1973, the Government announced the introduction of Industry Advisory Panels. These are aimed at enhancing liaison between Government and Industry and membership was to be drawn from representatives of industries, trade unions, consumers and the Australian Government. The first such Panel, the Textile and Apparel Industry Advisory Panel, held its inaugural meeting on 27th February, 1973.

411. It has not been necessary to lay down precise terms of reference for each Panel because the range of activities often varies according to the particular problems of the industry sectors concerned. However, broadly the responsibilities of Panels are those of:

- providing the Government with advice on policy matters concerning the industry,
- providing the liaison link between Government and industry to communicate information on industry trends and problems,
- informing the private sector of the Government's aims and objectives; and

- having regard to the Government's plans for future industrial development, assist to model and implement the future structure of the respective industry sectors.

Composition, Communication and Administration

412. As mentioned, the membership of Panels includes representatives of industry, trade unions, consumers and the Federal Government. The Secretary for the Department of Manufacturing Industry is the Chairman of each Panel and reports and recommendations are submitted to the Minister for Manufacturing Industry. The Secretariat for each Panel is provided by the Department of Manufacturing Industry and in all cases a departmental officer has been appointed as executive officer.

413. In selecting industry members the Minister looks to people who are engaged in business activities within the industry concerned. Such people usually hold a position of leadership within the industry which is often evidenced by their occupancy of a senior position in an industry association. This is intended to ensure that when questions of policy arise Panel members can express the views of the industry they represent and comment at first hand on issues under discussion. Provision is also made for alternative representation as well as observers from industry associations and organisations. The size of the Panels depends on the production range and size of the industries concerned. At present approximately 67% of all industry in terms of production is represented by Panels. (A list of existing Panels is shown in Table 6. 3. ).

Manufacturing Industries Advisory Council (MIAC)

414. The Manufacturing Industries Advisory Council was established by the then Minister for Trade in June 1958. The aim of setting up the Council was to bring together prominent businessmen - mainly manufacturers - to study the numerous problems associated with Australian development with particular reference to manufacturing industry. The Council was to provide objective and forward-thinking advice on how businessmen saw the current state of the economy, together with their views on possible ways of solving the problems inherent in growth. This advice was to be furnished, on a confidential basis, to the Minister (now the Minister for Manufacturing Industry) and through him to the Government.

415. At present members are selected by the Minister for Manufacturing Industry on the basis of the personal contribution they can make to the work of the Council and not as a representative of particular organisations, or business interests.

Machinery

416. In the past the membership of the full Council has been around 35 although it has fluctuated over the years, and at present there are 30 members. The Chairman of the Council is appointed by the Minister for Manufacturing Industry and since its formation in 1958 the Council has had three Chairmen. Members are appointed for an initial term of three years, and under normal circumstances are invited to serve for a further three years. Members appointed to the Steering Committee of the Council are usually invited to serve for a further three years, making nine years in all. Council membership also includes, as ex-officio members, the Secretary of the Department of Manufacturing Industry and the Secretary of the Department of Overseas Trade. The Council meets approximately every three months.

417. The Council appoints panels, which are in the nature of working committees, and are charged by the Council with the responsibility of studying and reporting on particular matters.

418. Some projects are originated by the Council itself whilst others are in the form of direct requests by the Minister for the Council's advice. An example of some of the major projects completed by the Council are set out in Table 6. 4.

419. In addition to specific projects undertaken by the Council, it regularly participates in consultative discussions with Government. In such discussions it presents its views on trends in manufacturing activity and the national economy.

Trade Development Council

420. Another form of Government-Industry dialogue is through the Trade Development Council previously known as the Export Development Council. The Council established in 1958 to advise the Australian Government on all aspects of the development of Australia's export trade is responsible to the Minister for Overseas Trade.

421. The structure of the Trade Development Council is similar to that of the Manufacturing Industries Advisory Council with panels set up to undertake the examination of particular subjects. In the past various sub-committees have been established to implement the work programme of the Council. However, these are no longer operative.

422. The Council has included in its work programme regular missions to new and potential overseas markets on which it prepares comprehensive reports on trade and investment opportunities for Australian industry. The Council also, at the invitation of the Prime Minister, meets with the Economic Committee of the Cabinet each year to discuss the current economic situation and to offer advice on ways and means to increase exports. At these meetings the Council is represented by the Chairman and a small group of representatives.

## Regional Offices

423. The Department of Manufacturing Industry has representatives in each State capital. These officers maintain regular contact with industry and ensure that current information is available to the Central Office.

## Co-operation and Communication with State Governments

424. Under the Australian system of Government each State maintains its own parliamentary system and legislative control over a wide range of activities. Such areas include company legislation, industrial development, and prices and wages policies. An inaugural meeting between Australian and State Government Ministers dealing specifically with industrial policy matters was held in April 1975. In addition to institutionalized meetings Ministers and their Departments do consult with State Ministers and their Departments on matters that have a direct bearing on industrial matters within those States, when this is appropriate.

425. Current areas where dialogue is taking place include: the development and implementation of a national urban and regional development strategy; assessment of the demand for transport services arising from initiatives in restructuring urban and regional areas; the formulation of a uniform companies' legislation; general employment issues including manpower training programmes; and the impact of structural change in decentralized areas.

## CONCLUSIONS

426. The present conclusions to the report on Australia's industrial policies start off by giving some indications as to the context in which Australian industry operates and the factors that have shaped its development. They then examine some of the major issues as they arise out of the report accompanied by practical considerations on some matters which the Industry Committee believed might be helpful to the Australian Authorities in the formulation or review of industrial policy.

427. Australian manufacturing industry developed in a country four-fifths the size of the United States, with a population slightly smaller than that of the Netherlands and an economy whose GNP is only a little bigger than that of Sweden.

428. Today, manufacturing industry employs 24% of the total work-force, contributes 24% of GDP, 13% of gross fixed capital expenditure, supplies over 20% of exports (largely basic metals and food products) and utilizes over 60% of all imports.

429. A number of special factors have influenced the profile of Australian industry, which can be summarized as follows:

- the existence of vast natural resources, the products of which are of a cyclically sensitive nature (exports of farm and mining products account for approximately 78% of the total).
- The large size and regional diversity of the Australian continent, which has tended to favour, despite major concentration in the south-eastern regions, fragmentation of industrial activity and involves heavy internal transport and communication costs.
- The relatively small population (population per sq. km. is the lowest of all OECD countries), which has provided a limited domestic market for manufacturers thus reducing their capability to engage in international competition.
- The relative geographical isolation of the Australian continent which involves transportation over long distances to export markets for products suitable for Australian producing capacity.
- The highly decentralized constitutional system in which powers to influence industrial development were long, and still largely are, allocated to the State Governments.

- The relatively large size of foreign investment in manufacturing industry, which, although it has led over the years to the creation and development of industries in Australia, may nevertheless not have contributed to the extent possible to the most efficient use of the country's resources.

430. Much of manufacturing industry in Australia was established and has grown under tariff protection. In fact, the tariff has been used as a major instrument to encourage industry to set up in Australia, although for most of the period between 1939 and 1960 import licensing also had a marked effect. However, since 1960, the tariff has been the only instrument (with a few exceptions) used by the Federal Government to influence specifically industrial development as distinct from measures of a general economic nature (e. g. taxation, demand management) which have helped shape the growth of industry generally by creating and influencing the environment within which industry operates. While tariff protection plays a major role through the level of assistance it provides to individual industries, it has also significantly influenced the movement of resources between industries. A given level of protection assists an industry to meet competition, mainly from overseas countries, and it also helps that industry to meet competition from other industries for available resources (e. g. materials, capital and labour) which it requires. Tariff protection therefore not only has a significant influence on the efficiency with which a given amount of resources is used in an industry, but also penalizes other industries which may be more competitive internationally, and thus require less or no tariff assistance in their bidding for limited resources.

431. These factors and others, such as those outlined in paragraph 429 above, have contributed to creating an industrial structure in which existing resources are used with less than optimal efficiency, thus reducing industry's contribution to national wealth. The Australian Government has become increasingly concerned about this situation as inefficiency in manufacturing industry not only impairs its international competitiveness but also contributes to reducing the Government's ability to pursue non-industrial objectives in fields such as transport and communication, health, environment, etc. , for the benefit of the community as a whole. To this end, the Government has announced its intention to put strong emphasis in the future on a more efficient use of the community's human and natural resources and to help industry to adapt to the changes required by the pursuit of this general objective at a pace that will take due account of the need to avoid disruption and social hardship. Examples of this policy are the endorsement of the tariff review begun in 1971 and of the policy guidelines set out in the Industries Assistance Commission Act. In addition the Government has appointed an Expert Committee, the Jackson Committee, to advise it on appropriate policies with regard to manufacturing

industry. The precise terms of reference of this Committee are set out in the report.

432. The report contains a number of indications as to the activities where Australia is best suited, where it has some cost or natural advantage or where cost disabilities are generally lower. This would indicate the desirability of concentrating on "low cost" industries, which implies a transfer of resources away from some "high cost" industries; development of industries based on the exploitation and, above all, the further processing of the natural resources which Australia possesses; encouragement of export-oriented industries; and the promotion of industries based on skill, innovation or design.

433. Policy directions such as those outlined above involve major restructuring of some sectors of industry. The Government is aware of the effort that structural adjustments on this scale will impose on the Australian community and has therefore introduced a permanent programme of adjustment assistance. This has since been supplemented by specific orientation programmes such as the programme of special assistance to non-metropolitan areas affected by structural change, which is also of particular importance in the context of Australia's regional development. The Industry Committee expressed its appreciation of the general change of emphasis, indicated in the report, away from the traditional, more protective attitude, as exemplified by the almost exclusive use of trade-directed measures, and towards an approach based on a growing use of adjustment assistance, as illustrated by the introduction of the above-mentioned programmes. It added that in the past trade-directed measures appear to have been used to achieve a number of objectives. Because of the broad nature of such measures it is likely that the particular objectives in mind have not been achieved in the most efficient manner. As reliance on trade-directed measures is reduced, efficient policy making requires the development of particular instruments which will enable the efficient achievement of the objectives broadly facilitated by trade-directed measures.

434. As these programmes have been introduced rather recently, it is not yet possible to assess their full impact and effectiveness. This fact helps explain the reasons that have impelled the Australian Government, in the light of falling-off of home demand and rapidly growing imports of some products, to introduce temporary import restraint measures intended to achieve stability in the short term so that rational re-structuring arrangements can be devised. The measures are primarily designed to contain the growth of imports and in very few cases only do quantitative restrictions apply. The products to which the import action relates represent also only a small proportion of total Australian manufactured imports. It is nevertheless important to underline that such measures may exert an unfavourable influence in

the present international economic and industrial environment. It is equally important that these measures be limited in their duration and their application to the requirements of a progressive and continuous adjustment in order to introduce or restore competitivity in the sectors concerned.

435. During the 1950's and for most of the 1960's import restrictions and tariffs respectively were used to build up manufacturing industry. This had the effect of insulating large sectors of manufacturing industry from the pressures of international competition and the need to adjust to them. Since the mid-1960's there has been a general recognition of the fact that assistance to manufacturing industry should be examined more closely to ensure that resources are being employed consistently with the objectives of government policy. As a result the level and incidence of the tariff, the major instrument of assistance to manufacturing industry, has been changing and in a number of cases very significantly especially since mid-1973. In essence, policy is being directed towards achieving a progressive and differentiated reduction of protection. The Industry Committee expresses support for the efforts of the Australian Government to formulate progressively a more coherent industrial policy geared towards long-term objectives. The required change in the direction of the tariff raises two fundamental questions (these questions being closely inter-related): first, speed and timing of reductions in the tariff; and, secondly, the role of adjustment assistance policies including policies designed to obtain the involvement of all segments of the community.

436. Of key importance in tariff reform in Australia is the Industries Assistance Commission which was established to advise the Government on developing co-ordinated policies for improving resource allocation; providing advice on those policies; and facilitating public scrutiny of those policies. A very important part of the Commission's work is concerned with the tariff review process which by 1978 will result in the review of assistance for the major sectors of manufacturing industry whose output is internationally traded. The review is designed to ensure that the operation of the tariff and other measures of assistance are more fully and consistently related to the Government's national objectives. The main means of doing this is by encouraging the development of, and flow of new investment into, the more - rather than the less - economic activities. The advisory body has said that it does not limit its judgement of whether an industry is economic to the level of assistance it requires in order to compete - it also considers a whole range of external benefits. The areas of the economy it sees being assisted by its approach are identified in a general way in its 1973/74 Annual Report, they are broadly speaking the areas identified in paragraph 432 above.

437. Experience in many countries tends to confirm that the efficacy of policies designed to change the existing industrial structure is

conditioned to a large extent by their ability to bring about a competitive environment in a way that provides a sufficiently strong incentive to enterprises to adapt while, at the same time, regulating the pace necessary for the change to take place in a socially and industrially acceptable manner. Such an approach implies that reductions in the tariff are introduced in a gradual way in respect of both the industries which are affected and the way the level of the tariff is changed. It also implies that the level of structural change is related to the general capacity of the economy to sustain such change. It is clear that during a period of reduced economic activity, when unemployment and employment maintenance problems come to the fore, the capacity of the economy to sustain structural change is accordingly lowered.

438. As well as the need to pay close attention to the timing of changes in the extent to which industries are exposed to increased competitive pressures in the sense mentioned in the previous paragraph, there is also a need for supporting adjustment assistance policies so that change can be consolidated. The need for such policies has been recognized by the Australian Government and a comprehensive Structural Adjustment Assistance Scheme has been established. Some of the institutional arrangements associated with the scheme are still being developed. This scheme provides a range of assistance to individuals, firms and regions affected by particular structural changes, especially tariff changes. It is aimed at increasing the economy's adaptive capacity and ensuring that the costs of socially desirable changes do not fall disproportionately on particular groups.

439. In addition to the structural adjustment assistance policies outlined above, which are to a considerable extent aimed at encouraging industries to adjust out of uneconomic lines of production, there is also a need to complement these policies with anticipatory measures designed to encourage resources to flow into areas of relatively greater advantage. Greater emphasis therefore should be placed on forward-looking measures directed, for example, towards encouraging research and innovation, greater efficiency and productivity, and the development of high quality resources. Such a strategy, in terms of aggregate costs and benefits to the community, would appear to be more desirable than an approach which relies essentially on reactive measures.

440. Apart from unilateral tariff changes, pressure will be placed on the adaptive capacity of the economy and manufacturing industry in particular by, amongst other things, the possible results of the multilateral trade negotiations at present under way, the increasing competitive strength in a widening range of manufactured goods of the countries within Australia's geographical region and the possibilities offered by the Australia-New Zealand Free Trade Agreement. Together with changes generated in response to purely domestic considerations, these elements will place significant demands on the adaptive capacity

of the Australian economy which will require the existence of well developed programmes to facilitate such changes.

441. The Australian Government has recognized that change, especially when brought about by change in existing measures of national support, requires the involvement and co-operation of all segments of the Australian community if the desired objectives are to be achieved in an acceptable manner. Early in the life of the present Australian Government steps were taken to establish a series of industry panels composed of members of industry, unions and consumers to advise the Minister for Manufacturing Industry. Such panels, if they are to realize their potential in relation to the process of industrial development rather than to be concerned primarily with the maintenance of the status quo, need to have a strong emphasis on longer term perspectives. Also of importance in the process of achieving involvement in the development of policies towards industrial development are the procedures of the Industries Assistance Commission. While the modus operandi of the Commission is essentially that of a Tribunal it has nevertheless moved to open up a greater dialogue with industry by publishing the recommendations and analysis of its most recent important manufacturing industry report in draft form. This desirable step, if generalized, should increase the community's involvement in the work of the Commission and contribute to the achievement of the level of consensus necessary for effective policy making.

442. As stated in the report, Australia's industrial policy should be viewed as being complementary to and closely interrelated with other economic policies. This approach points to an important concept of industrial policy: that of policy coherence to be achieved, in this case, largely through close co-ordination. The development of industry is profoundly affected by policies shaping general economic conditions (taxes, tariffs, exchange rates, etc. ), industry location and industry structure, and resource utilization. These policies are under the jurisdiction, as is the case in many other countries, of a number of different federal departments. An important function of a Department responsible for manufacturing industry is to advise the Government on all matters relating to the section so that the Government in taking decisions is aware of the possible implications for industry. This implies that a Department of Manufacturing Industry should be aware of policies being developed by other Departments in order to ensure that industrial policy considerations are duly taken into account. But it also implies (and more importantly) that a Department of Manufacturing Industry can suggest ways where policy instruments administered by other Departments could take into account the needs of manufacturing industry. This need for coherence is the more crucial in the Australian context as, mainly for traditional reasons, a number of policy instruments are administered by largely autonomous boards responsible to different Government departments. The risks exists,

in these cases, that the action by these boards may be largely reactive and may thus run counter to the need for a more anticipatory approach, in particular with regard to industrial adjustment. The question may be raised as to whether it would not be advisable to examine alternative possibilities to instil greater coherence and a more forward-looking approach into the administration of these instruments.

443. Co-ordination of the relevant government policy instruments, e. g. industrial, manpower, regional, environment, science policies, appears to be among the conditions for promoting the maximum reconciliation of objectives. In other words, goal conflicts in industrial adjustment policies are inevitable. There exists therefore a need for procedures for determining the likely consequences of different policy alternatives. While, to some extent, the standing Interdepartmental Committees can contribute to reducing the areas of conflict, it must be realized that, beyond a given point, the necessary trade-offs can only be made at the relevant political level. An interesting experiment in this respect has been carried out in France where a Cabinet Committee is responsible for the study and co-ordination of industrial policy problems and activities. More specifically, it is responsible for examining industrial policy problems of common interest, for co-ordinating specific industrial policy measures undertaken by the different departments concerned, for proposing measures to encourage medium and long-term industrial development. Chaired by the Prime Minister or in his absence by the Minister for Industry, the Committee brings together ministers whose departmental responsibilities have some bearing on industrial policy. In the Australian context this possibility could be viewed as a complement to the Economic Cabinet Committee where important overall economic matters, both structural and conjunctural, may overshadow industrial policy considerations in the examination of proposals submitted to them.

444. The Australian Government attaches great importance to improved communications among Government (Federal and State) and private business, organised labour and other segments of the community (e. g. consumers), as it is primarily through the actions of the private sector that industrial policies are implemented. It is therefore of importance that all the relevant partners be involved through appropriate consultative and advisory arrangements at an early stage in the formulation of industry policies in order to ensure a level of common thinking and acceptance. As mentioned above, a major step in this direction was the setting up in early 1973, i. e. shortly after the creation of the Department of Secondary Industry (later to become the Department of Manufacturing Industry), of Industry Advisory Panels which now exist for most major industries. An effort to restructure industry such as that envisaged in Australia implies the movement of resources from one sector to another, from one activity to another. A series of policy issues arises in this process,

which either relate to individual factors of production (natural resources, manpower, capital) or to various other aspects of production, (e. g. productivity), innovation, industrial design, export marketing and small business). In each of these areas also opportunities need to be identified and performance improved through appropriate policies. Such questions need to be examined from the point of view of the needs and the interests of industry as a whole, as opposed to an exclusively sectoral point of view.

445. The MIAC,* with a changed and enlarged membership modelled on the composition of Industry Advisory Panels and acting in a more public fashion, could fulfil a quadruple function in this context: (1) provide a forum for representatives of all interested segments of the community to express their views on industry policy matters within a longer term perspective; (2) advise the Government on industry policy objectives and appropriate measures to achieve these objectives; (3) co-ordinate and guide the work of the Industry Advisory Panels with a view to integrate their activities in a wider overall industrial policy framework; (4) initiate and undertake any research work or studies and collect any information it considers necessary to enable it to fulfil its functions efficiently. The Council should preferably be chaired by an independent personality and be serviced by an autonomous Secretariat. It would report to the Minister for Manufacturing Industries. The need for the existence of such a superimposed body with an overall industry perspective and concentrating on long-term development would seem to be particularly apparent in Australia as, contrary to the situation prevailing in other countries, the habit of and machinery for consultation and co-operation at this level between the Government, business, organised labour, consumer and academic circles, seems to be lacking. Insofar as industrial policies are implemented largely through the private sector, as mentioned above, consultation at an early stage in the formulation of policies largely conditions their effectiveness at the implementing stage. Specialized advisory councils on industrial policy matters exist, for example, in Japan and Sweden.

446. The availability of long-term investment capital at an economic cost is an important factor in industrial development. Strong competition between different parts of the economy for limited long-term funds generated domestically in relation to the large number and size of opportunities in Australia (hence the traditional reliance on the inflow of foreign capital) make this question particularly crucial in the Australian context. Investment needs over the next decade or so include major new investments in processing and manufacturing facilities, in the development and transportation of natural resources and in those industries which are export-oriented or based on innovation

* Manufacturing Industry Advisory Council.

and skill. To the extent that the Government's policy reduces the level of foreign direct investment, it will be important for the available capital, either domestic or foreign, to be directed to the most productive utilization. The recently introduced amendments to the statute of the AIDC* should contribute to the widening of the choices open with regard to investment financing sources.

447. The policy of the Australian Government with regard to foreign investment is based on general principles which were first outlined by the Prime Minister in November 1973. The policy is being applied in a pragmatic way and each case is examined on its merits. This case by case approach constitutes a continuing study. The Australian Government believes that any uncertainties which may have existed about foreign takeovers policy were resolved by a statement by the Treasurer on 10th December, 1974 which detailed the Government's policy proposals for comprehensive foreign takeovers legislation. The Industry Committee hoped that the Australian Government would, when formulating future policies in this field, take due account of the desirability of avoiding measures which may have a distorting effect on capital inflows or discriminate against foreign-owned or controlled enterprises already established in Australia.

448. Within the framework of the efforts undertaken by the Australian Government to upgrade the level of local processing of export products, particularly minerals, in line with its decentralization strategy, the industrial complexes of the Pilbara type constitute an interesting experiment. If all the projects at present under active consideration by State and Federal authorities are implemented, they could ultimately have a considerable effect on the pattern of Australia's external trade, its industrial structures and those of its trading partners.

449. The Australian Government is also concerned to improve efficiency and productivity in industry generally, and small business in particular, through a number of programmes, e. g. management education, interfirm comparisons, research and development. In the light of the emphasis to be put on the development of industries based on innovation and skills and the role played by industrial technology as a resource for industrial growth generally, the policies pursued by the Australian Government in this area, and in particular the Industrial Research and Development Grants Acts of 1969, merit particular attention. This instrument is at present undergoing a comprehensive review. As already indicated above, effective adjustment to complex patterns of economic and technological change, even within a single sector, would often seem to require the utilization of a combination of different instruments directed towards a given industrial policy objective. It is therefore important that the instruments be shaped in a way

* Australian Industry Development Corporation.

that will allow for maximum flexibility in their utilization, taking into account the diversity of needs they may be called upon to serve.

450. The National Small Business Bureau, set up by the Government as part of the SMB Programme, could contribute, among its many functions, to making SMB managers more aware of the importance of industrial innovation and R and D. The range of services offered by this body needs to be comprehensive if it is to be effective, since SMB's do not have the time to consult large numbers of different bodies, which might well proffer differing information or advice. Close contacts between industry and the National Bureau constitute another condition of its success. It would be useful for a service of this kind to operate on a mainly decentralized basis, with independent antennae in parts of Australia with large numbers of SMB's or high development potential. Although it is not at this stage the intention to provide the National Bureau with financing resources and functions, it should however, be emphasized that the requirements of SMB's, whatever their area of activity or their stage of development, are also of a financial nature, and it is important that existing financial facilities meet the requirements of small business. The Swedish example of BDA's* can be quoted in this connection.

451. Limited mention only is made in the report of the collection and exchange of information generally on present developments and policies and, in particular, of information related to expectations and intentions. In order to enable the policymakers to devise policies of an anticipatory nature destined to act more on industrial development opportunities, as distinguished from "problems", and the advisory and consultative bodies to give informed advice on them, particular attention needs to be paid to forecasting the nature and extent of structural changes. Existing procedures of an advisory and consultative nature (e. g. the MIAC in its present or amended form, the IAP's, etc. ) should therefore be examined to determine to what extent the present scope of their function needs to be developed in order to take due account of this particularly important need.

* Business Development Association.

# STATISTICAL APPENDIX

## AUSTRIALIA

**PERCENTAGE OF LABOUR FORCE IN EACH STATE ENGAGED IN MANUFACTURE (AS AT 30 JUNE 1971)**

MANUFACTURING WORKFORCE IN MAJOR CENTRES OF POPULATION

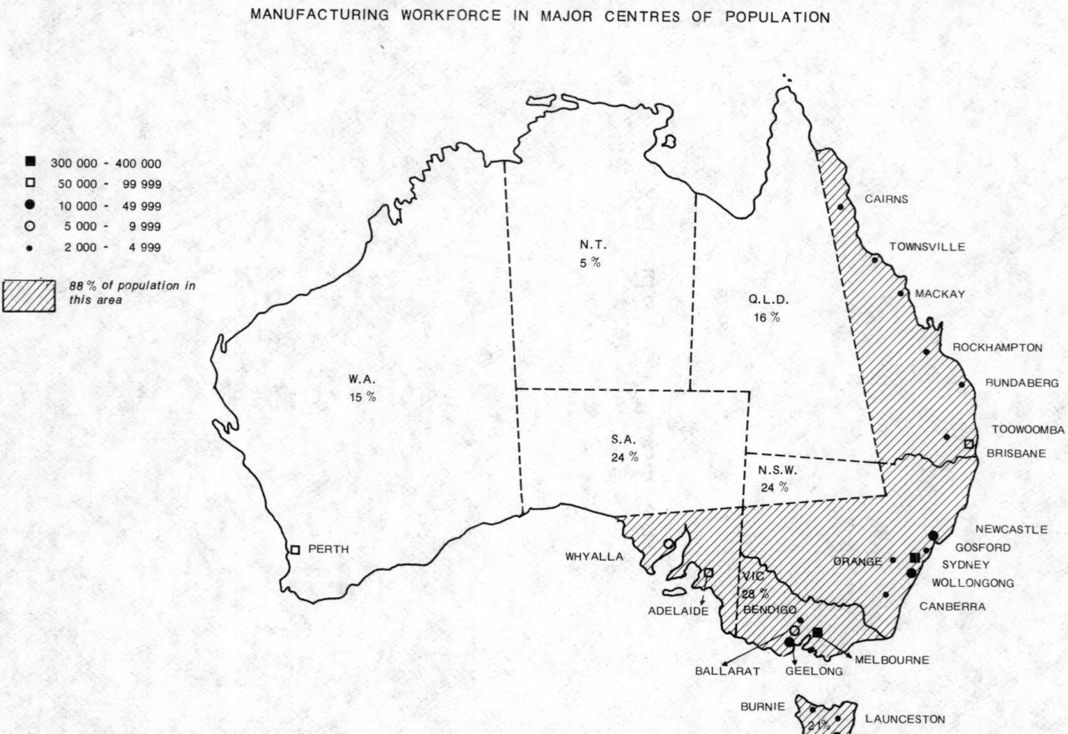


Based on 1971 census conducted by the Australian Bureau of Statistics.

Table 2. 1. DISTRIBUTION OF EMPLOYMENT[a] AND VALUE ADDED BY INDUSTRY SUBDIVISIONS BY STATE AS % OF TOTAL AUSTRALIA
1972/73

| INDUSTRY SUBDIVISION | ASPECT | NSW | VIC | QLD | SA | WA | TAS | TOTAL[b] |
|---|---|---|---|---|---|---|---|---|
| Food, Beverages and Tobacco | Value added | 30. 7 | 34. 0 | 17. 6 | 7. 8 | 6. 0 | 3. 4 | 100 |
| | Employment | 32. 2 | 31. 5 | 16. 8 | 9. 2 | 6. 8 | 2. 9 | 100 |
| Textiles | Value added | 32. 3 | 53. 6 | 2. 6 | 4. 6 | 1. 6 | 5. 4 | 100 |
| | Employment | 30. 0 | 53. 4 | 3. 7 | 4. 7 | 1. 3 | 6. 9 | 100 |
| Clothing and Footwear | Value added | 34. 4 | 56. 0 | 4. 2 | 4. 0 | 1. 2 | 0. 2 | 100 |
| | Employment | 34. 0 | 54. 3 | 5. 9 | 3. 9 | 1. 5 | 0. 3 | 100 |
| Wood, Wood Products and Furniture | Value added | 35. 1 | 24. 4 | 15. 1 | 9. 1 | 8. 9 | 6. 9 | 100 |
| | Employment | 33. 2 | 25. 4 | 15. 7 | 10. 0 | 9. 4 | 5. 7 | 100 |
| Paper, Paper Products and Printing | Value added | 40. 2 | 33. 1 | 7. 9 | 7. 3 | 4. 8 | 5. 2 | 100 |
| | Employment | 39. 3 | 33. 1 | 8. 9 | 6. 7 | 5. 4 | 5. 3 | 100 |
| Chemical, Petroleum and Coal Products | Value added | 51. 9 | 30. 1 | 6. 4 | 4. 2 | 5. 4 | 1. 9 | 100 |
| | Employment | 49. 1 | 34. 6 | 4. 7 | 4. 6 | 4. 8 | 2. 2 | 100 |
| Non-Metallic Mineral Products | Value added | 39. 1 | 27. 4 | 13. 1 | 8. 2 | 8. 7 | 2. 3 | 100 |
| | Employment | 41. 0 | 28. 1 | 11. 6 | 7. 9 | 8. 4 | 2. 0 | 100 |
| Basic Metal Products | Value added | 61. 1 | 11. 0 | 10. 0 | 9. 6 | 1. 9 | 5. 1 | 100 |
| | Employment | 61. 3 | 13. 2 | 5. 0 | 10. 3 | 5. 2 | 4. 0 | 100 |
| Fabricated Metal Products | Value added | 38. 6 | 35. 0 | 9. 7 | 8. 9 | 6. 2 | 1. 1 | 100 |
| | Employment | 38. 9 | 33. 5 | 10. 1 | 9. 5 | 6. 3 | 1. 2 | 100 |
| Transport Equipment | Value added | 30. 4 | 42. 9 | 8. 5 | 14. 4 | 2. 7 | 0. 9 | 100 |
| | Employment | 30. 5 | 39. 8 | 8. 3 | 17. 4 | 3. 1 | 0. 8 | 100 |
| Other Machinery and Equipment | Value added | 44. 0 | 38. 2 | 4. 2 | 9. 8 | 3. 1 | 0. 5 | 100 |
| | Employment | 44. 4 | 36. 2 | 4. 5 | 10. 9 | 3. 4 | 0. 6 | 100 |
| Miscellaneous Manufacturing | Value added | 40. 7 | 44. 8 | 4. 8 | 7. 2 | 2. 3 | 0. 3 | 100 |
| | Employment | 39. 8 | 43. 7 | 5. 4 | 8. 0 | 2. 7 | 0. 4 | 100 |
| Total Manufacturing | Value added | 39. 9 | 34. 5 | 9. 6 | 8. 4 | 4. 5 | 2. 6 | 100 |
| | Employment | 38. 8 | 35. 3 | 8. 9 | 9. 4 | 4. 8 | 2. 4 | 100 |

SOURCE: Australian Bureau of Statistics Census of Manufacturing Establishments 1972/73 - Preliminary Statement.

a) Average over whole year, including working proprietors.

b) Figures may not add to 100% due to absence of Australian Capital Territory and Northern Territory from the table.

Table 2. 2. SECTORAL CONTRIBUTION TO GROSS DOMESTIC PRODUCT AS A PERCENTAGE OF TOTAL GROSS DOMESTIC PRODUCT - SELECTED COUNTRIES
1972

| | % | | |
|---|---|---|---|
| | AGRICULTURE | MANUFACTURING | ALL OTHER INDUSTRIES INCLUDING SERVICES SECTOR |
| Australia[a] ........... | 6. 4 | 23. 6 | 70. 0 |
| Canada .............. | 3. 6 | 20. 4 | 76. 0 |
| United Kingdom ....... | 2. 5 | 27. 2 | 70. 2 |
| United States of America ........... | 3. 0 | 25. 2 | 71. 8 |
| Japan ............... | 5. 8 | 33. 0 | 61. 2 |
| France .............. | 6. 2 | 36. 1[b] | 57. 7[c] |
| Italy ................ | 8. 0 | 31. 3 | 60. 7 |

SOURCE: U.N. Monthly Bulletin of Statistics, July 1974.

a) Refers to financial year 1971/72.
b) Includes mining and electricity, gas and water.
c) Excludes mining and electricity, gas and water.

Table 2. 3. GROWTH OF VALUE ADDED IN THE FOOD, BEVERAGES AND TOBACCO SECTOR BETWEEN 1968/69 AND 1972/73

| FOOD, BEVERAGES AND TOBACCO INDUSTRY CLASS | VALUE ADDED IN | | PERCENTAGE GROWTH |
|---|---|---|---|
| | 1968/69 | 1972/73 | |
| Meat Products | 240. 5 | 506. 1 | 110 |
| Milk Products | 157. 7 | 217. 9 | 38 |
| Fruit and Vegetables | 94. 0 | 146. 8 | 56 |
| Margarine and Oil Fats | 23. 8 | 40. 6 | 71 |
| Flour Mill and Cereal Products | 72. 4 | 93. 3 | 29 |
| Bread, Cakes and Biscuits | 157. 0 | 212. 3 | 35 |
| Sugar<br>Other Food Products | 193. 7 | 311. 6 | 61 |
| Beverages and Malt | 172. 8 | 289. 9 | 68 |
| Tobacco Products | 72. 5 | 126. 5 | 74 |
| Total Food, Beverages and Tobacco | 1, 184. 4 | 1, 945. 1 | 64 |

SOURCE: Australian Bureau of Statistics, Census of Manufacturing Establishments, 1972/73.

Table 2. 4. TARIFFS AND INDUSTRY GROWTH RATES

| INDUSTRY GROUP | AVERAGE NOMINAL RATE 1969/1970 | AVERAGE EFFECTIVE RATE 1969/1970 | % GROWTH IN VALUE ADDED 1969/70-1972/73 |
|---|---|---|---|
| Food, Beverages, Tobacco | 9 | 11 | 46 |
| Textiles | 23 | 41 | 24 |
| Clothing and Footwear | 45 | 83 | 23 |
| Wood, Wood Products, Furniture | 21 | 26 | 35 |
| Paper, paper products, Printing | 28 | 50 | 32 |
| Chemical, petroleum, Coal products | 24 | 37 | 32 |
| Non-metallic mineral Products | 12 | 15 | 39 |
| Basic metal products | 14 | 29 | 21 |
| Fabricated Metal Products | 39 | 73 | 27 |
| Transport Equipment | 38 | 57 | 16 |
| Other machinery and Equipment | 32 | 44 | 23 |
| Miscellaneous Manufacturing | 29 | 38 | 45 |
| Manufacturing Sector | 22 | 35 | 30 |

SOURCE: Derived from Appendix 3.4 of the 1973/74 Industries Assistance Commission Annual Report and the Australian Bureau of Commission Annual Report and the Australian Bureau of Statistics Manufacturing Establishment Bulletin.

Table 2.5. EMPLOYMENT BY MANUFACTURING INDUSTRY GROUP
(Average over whole year)[a)]

| INDUSTRY SUBDIVISION | MALES | | FEMALES | | TOTAL NUMBERS | | TOTAL AS % | |
|---|---|---|---|---|---|---|---|---|
| | 1968/69 | 1972/73 | 1968/69 | 1972/73 | 1968/69 | 1972/73 | 1968/69 | 1972/73 |
| Food Beverages and Tobacco | 137,139 | 150,250 | 47,667 | 55,851 | 184,806 | 206,101 | 14.6 | 15.7 |
| Textiles Clothing and Footwear | 58,981 | 55,008 | 121,838 | 111,840 | 180,819 | 166,848 | 14.3 | 12.7 |
| Wood, Wood Products and Furniture | 73,931 | 72,360 | 9,140 | 11,006 | 83,071 | 83,336 | 6.6 | 6.4 |
| Paper, Paper Products and Printing | 73,732 | 77,832 | 27,833 | 29,933 | 101,565 | 107,765 | 8.0 | 8.2 |
| Chemical, Petroleum and Coal Products | 46,960 | 47,770 | 16,804 | 17,646 | 63,764 | 65,416 | 5.0 | 5.0 |
| Non-Metallic Mineral Products | 46,331 | 47,527 | 4,783 | 5,574 | 51,114 | 53,101 | 4.0 | 4.1 |
| Basic Metal Products | 83,299 | 89,592 | 4,941 | 6,331 | 88,240 | 95,923 | 7.0 | 7.3 |
| Transport Equipment | 131,217 | 136,984 | 13,297 | 16,917 | 144,514 | 153,901 | 11.4 | 11.8 |
| Fabricated Metal Products and Other Machinery and Equipment | 234,789 | 232,065 | 65,970 | 70,831 | 300,759 | 302,896 | 23.8 | 23.1 |
| Other Manufacturing | 43,592 | 48,263 | 21,793 | 25,152 | 65,385 | 73,415 | 5.2 | 5.6 |
| TOTAL | 929,971 | 957,651 | 334,066 | 351,081 | 1,264,037 | 1,308,732 | 100.0 | 100.0 |

SOURCES: Australian Bureau of Statistics, Manufacturing Establishments - Details of Operation by Industry Class, Australia 1968/69.
Australian Bureau of Statistics, Census of Manufacturing Establishments 1972/73 - Preliminary Statement.

a) Including working proprietors.

Table 2.6. CHANGES IN LABOUR PRODUCTIVITY IN MANUFACTURING INDUSTRY[a)]
(Average percentage change per annum)

| | AUSTRALIA | BRITAIN | CANADA | FRANCE | FED. REP. OF GERMANY | ITALY | JAPAN | UNITED STATES OF AMERICA |
|---|---|---|---|---|---|---|---|---|
| 1961/62 to 1970/71[b)] | 3.6 | 3.9 | 3.6 | 6.2 | 5.1 | 5.6 | 11.7 | 2.8 |
| 1969/70 to 1972/73 | 3.2 | 3.9 | 3.7 | 8.3 | 3.1 | 0.4 | 8.4 | 2.4 |
| 1971/72 to 1972/73 | 5.6 | 5.7 | 4.5 | 10.5 | 2.7 | 3.0 | 4.9 | 2.7 |

SOURCE: Australian Tariff Board Annual Report 1970/71, 1972/73.

a) Labour productivity index = $\frac{\text{Index of volume of manufacturing (of factory production)}}{\text{Index of total man hours in manufacturing.}}$

where total man hours = number of employees in manufacturing multiplied by estimated average hours of work per employee in manufacturing.

b) The period 1961/62 - 1970/71 is not strictly comparable to the two later periods.

Table 2. 7. FIXED CAPITAL EXPENDITURE IN SELECTED INDUSTRIES 1968/69-1972/73

| INDUSTRY | 1968/69 | 1969/70 | 1971/72 | 1972/73 | CHANGE 1968/69-1972/73 |
|---|---|---|---|---|---|
| | $ million | | | | % |
| Textiles .............................. | 29. 7 | 41. 5 | 28. 7 | 24. 9 | -16. 0 |
| Clothing and Footwear ................ | 19. 4 | 20. 3 | 18. 7 | 19. 5 | 0. 5 |
| Basic Metal Products ................ | 175. 1 | 238. 2 | 444. 3 | 330. 6 | 89. 0 |
| Fabricated Metal Products ............ | 52. 6 | 54. 4 | 62. 7 | 56. 4 | 7. 0 |
| Transport Equipment ................ | 89. 8 | 104. 1 | 135. 7 | 112. 3 | 25. 0 |
| Other machinery and equipment ....... | 80. 6 | 82. 0 | 91. 1 | 95. 0 | 18. 0 |

SOURCE: Australian Bureau of Statistics, Census of Manufacturing Establishments 1972/73.

Table 2.8. OVERSEAS OWNERSHIP AND CONTROL OF INDIVIDUAL MANUFACTURING INDUSTRIES, 1966-67

| | VALUE OF PRODUCTION ATTRIBUTABLE TO: a) | | AVERAGE EMPLOYMENT ATTRIBUTABLE TO: | |
|---|---|---|---|---|
| | OVERSEAS OWNERSHIP b) | OVERSEAS CONTROL | OVERSEAS OWNERSHIP b) | OVERSEAS CONTROL |
| | (% OF TOTAL) | (% OF TOTAL) | (% OF TOTAL) | (% OF TOTAL) |
| Motor vehicles, construction and assembly | 88.3 | 87.8 | 88.6 | 87.3 |
| Non-ferrous metals-rolling and extrusion | 62.4 | 83.6 | 60.9 | 82.9 |
| Oils, mineral | 79.5 | 81.6 | 77.3 | 80.7 |
| Industrial and heavy chemicals, acids | 58.7 | 78.0 | 54.7 | 76.4 |
| Pharmaceutical and toilet preparations | 75.1 | 76.3 | 58.1 | 59.4 |
| White lead, paints, varnishes | 57.3 | 69.6 | 53.0 | 65.6 |
| Musical instruments | 65.2 | 65.2 | 35.3 | 35.3 |
| Other chemicals | 51.5 | 58.2 | 39.8 | 47.8 |
| Wireless and amplifying apparatus | 39.3 | 46.2 | 38.8 | 44.0 |
| Electrical machinery, cables and apparatus | 36.0 | 42.4 | 34.6 | 40.1 |
| Agricultural machines and implements | 32.0 | 32.3 | 32.0 | 32.1 |
| Other food, drink and tobacco | 24.0 | 30.9 | 20.9 | 25.2 |
| Meat and fish preserving | 29.8 | 30.8 | 31.5 | 32.6 |
| Jam, fruit and vegetable canning | 26.2 | 28.7 | 22.5 | 24.9 |
| Rubber | 22.3 | 23.1 | 21.6 | 22.5 |
| Plant, equipment and machinery | 19.3 | 22.1 | 16.3 | 19.2 |
| Other industrial metals, etc. | 16.5 | 21.5 | 13.9 | 17.1 |
| Miscellaneous products | 17.0 | 20.0 | 16.3 | 18.7 |
| Textiles and textile goods (not dress) | 13.5 | 15.5 | 13.9 | 15.7 |
| Bakeries (including cakes and pastry) | 11.5 | 14.5 | 8.5 | 10.6 |
| Paper, stationery, printing, bookbinding, etc. | 10.7 | 13.8 | 7.5 | 9.7 |
| Treatment of non-metalli-ferous mine and quarry products | 9.4 | 11.5 | 7.9 | 9.6 |
| Bricks, pottery, glass, etc. | 10.5 | 10.1 | 8.7 | 8.6 |
| Clothing (except knitted) | 4.2 | 6.1 | 3.7 | 5.0 |
| Sawmills, joinery, boxes, etc. | 4.7 | 5.4 | 3.6 | 4.2 |
| Furniture of wood, bedding, etc. | 2.9 | 4.7 | 2.3 | 3.6 |
| Skins and leather (not clothing or footwear) | 4.4 | 4.7 | 3.5 | 3.8 |
| Heat, light and power | 0.6 | 0.8 | 1.2 | 1.5 |
| Total | 22.2 | 26.3 | 17.5 | 20.5 |

a) The value of production is the value added to materials by the process of manufacture.
b) Excludes ownership resulting from overseas portfolio investment.

Table 2.9. PROFITABILITY: MANUFACTURING SECTOR

| RATIOS | 1965/66 % | 1966/67 % | 1967/68 % | 1968/69 % | 1969/70 % | 1970/71 % | 1971/72 % | 1972/73 % |
|---|---|---|---|---|---|---|---|---|
| Operating profit/ Funds employed | 10.2 | 10.6 | 11.4 | 12.6 | 13.0 | 12.1 | 11.5 | 13.0 |
| Operating profit/ Sales | 7.1 | 7.3 | 7.8 | 8.4 | 8.4 | 7.8 | 7.5 | 8.0 |
| Net profit/ Sales | 3.8 | 4.0 | 4.2 | 4.7 | 4.5 | 4.3 | 4.2 | 4.7 |
| Net profit/paid-up capital | 15.1 | 16.1 | 18.8 | 21.6 | 22.2 | 22.7 | 21.9 | 27.4 |
| Net profit/Share-holders funds | 6.6 | 7.0 | 7.7 | 9.5 | 9.6 | 9.6 | 9.0 | 11.1 |
| Dividends paid/ Net profit | 56.5 | 55.3 | 53.1 | 49.3 | 53.1 | 51.9 | 53.5 | 49.1 |
| Dividends paid/ Paid-up capital | 8.5 | 8.9 | 10.0 | 10.6 | 11.8 | 11.8 | 11.7 | 13.5 |

SOURCE: Australian Tariff Board Annual Report 1972-73 and 1973/74.

Table 2.10. PROFITABILITY RATIOS 1970/71-1972/73

| | | 1970-71 % | 1971-72 % | 1972-73 % |
|---|---|---|---|---|
| Textiles, yarns and woven products | Op. profit/funds | 10.5 | 9.3 | 12.4 |
| | Op. profit/sales | 7.2 | 6.5 | 7.4 |
| Floor coverings and other textile products | Op. profit/funds | 12.7 | 12.4 | 18.3 |
| | Op. profit/sales | 7.0 | 6.8 | 8.8 |
| Knitting mills and clothing | Op. profit/funds | 15.3 | 14.6 | 18.9 |
| | Op. profit/sales | 6.1 | 5.6 | 7.4 |
| Footwear | Op. profit/funds | 19.0 | 16.6 | 21.7 |
| | Op. profit/sales | 6.3 | 5.4 | 6.7 |
| Fabricated metal products | Op. profit/funds | 13.4 | 12.6 | 15.0 |
| | Op. profit/sales | 8.6 | 7.6 | 7.6 |
| Motor vehicles, bodies trailers and caravans | Op. profit/funds | 13.0 | 7.8 | 6.5 |
| | Op. profit/sales | 6.4 | 3.5 | 2.7 |
| Motor vehicle instruments parts, accessories | Op. profit/funds | 14.4 | 14.6 | 16.5 |
| | Op. profit/sales | 9.4 | 9.7 | 10.5 |
| Other transport equipment | Op. profit/funds | 12.6 | 10.1 | 8.3 |
| | Op. profit/sales | 4.8 | 4.2 | 3.0 |
| Industrial machinery and equipment | Op. profit/funds | 13.0 | 12.4 | 13.6 |
| | Op. profit/sales | 7.6 | 6.9 | 7.6 |
| Total Manufacturing | Op. profit/funds | 12.1 | 11.5 | 13.0 |
| | Op. profit/sales | 7.8 | 7.5 | 8.0 |

SOURCE: Derived from data in Table 4.2.3. of the Industries Assistance Commission Annual Report 1973/74.

Table 2.11. ESTABLISHMENTS, EMPLOYMENT, TURNOVER AND VALUE ADDED OF MANUFACTURING ESTABLISHMENTS ACCORDING TO EMPLOYMENT SIZE AT 30 JUNE 1969

| SIZE OF ESTABLISHMENT (No. EMPLOYED) | No. OF ESTABLISHMENTS | % OF ESTABLISHMENTS | % OF EMPLOYMENT (INCL. WORKING PROPRIETORS) | % OF TURNOVER | % OF VALUE ADDED |
|---|---|---|---|---|---|
| 1 - 9 ............. | 20,282 | 56.4 | 7.0 | 5.3 | 5.6 |
| 10 - 49 ............. | 11,191 | 31.1 | 19.7 | 16.8 | 17.0 |
| 50 - 99 ............. | 2,077 | 5.8 | 11.8 | 12.2 | 11.5 |
| 100 - 499 ............. | 2,089 | 5.8 | 33.9 | 36.4 | 35.4 |
| 500 - 999 ............. | 196 | 0.5 | 10.7 | 11.0 | 11.6 |
| 1,000 - and over ........ | 104 | 0.3 | 17.0 | 18.4 | 18.8 |
| | 35,939 | 100.0 | 100.0 | 100.0 | 100.0 |

SOURCE: Australian Bureau of Statistics - Manufacturing Establishments, Selected Items of Data.

Table 2.12. LARGEST 20 ENTERPRISE GROUPS AS PROPORTION TO TOTAL INDUSTRY SUB-DIVISIONS (1968-69)

(%)

| INDUSTRY SUB-DIVISIONS | ESTABLISHMENTS | TURNOVER | VALUE ADDED | EMPLOYMENT END JUNE 1969 |
|---|---|---|---|---|
| Food, beverages and tobacco | 7 | 33 | 33 | 31 |
| Textiles | 11 | 57 | 56 | 50 |
| Clothing and footwear | 4 | 27 | 24 | 20 |
| Wood, wood products and furniture | 2 | 19 | 18 | 15 |
| Paper, paper products and printing | 4 | 47 | 43 | 36 |
| Chemical, petroleum and coal products | 10 | 52 | 51 | 44 |
| Non-metallic mineral products | 23 | 59 | 60 | 53 |
| Basic metal products | 18 | 87 | 85 | 80 |
| Fabricated metal products | 4 | 30 | 26 | 22 |
| Transport equipment | 6 | 73 | 69 | 62 |
| Other machinery and equipment | 2 | 27 | 24 | 25 |
| Miscellaneous manufacturing | 4 | 48 | 45 | 37 |
| Total manufacturing | 2 | 22 | 19 | 15 |

SOURCE: Australian Bureau of Statistics: Industry Concentration Statistics 1968/69.

Table 2.13. EXPORTS OF MANUFACTURING (INCLUDING RE-EXPORTS)
(Value $m f.o.b. and percentage of total)

| | 1966/67 | 1967/68 | 1968/69 | 1969/70 | 1970/71 | 1971/72 | 1972/73 (p) |
|---|---|---|---|---|---|---|---|
| Iron and Steel ......... | 117.6 (3.9) | 96.2 (3.1) | 108.0 (3.2) | 136.0 (3.3) | 90.8 (2.1) | 106.2 (2.2) | 164.0 (2.6) |
| Petroleum ........... | 30.4 (1.0) | 33.2 (1.1) | 26.4 (0.8) | 27.7 (0.7) | 41.6 (1.0) | 60.2 (1.2) | 46.5 (0.8) |
| Vehicles and parts .... | 58.8 (1.9) | 57.8 (1.9) | 72.1 (2.1) | 123.9 (3.0) | 134.8 (3.1) | 159.3 (3.3) | 254.8 (4.1) |
| Machinery and elect. equipment ........... | 83.7 (2.8) | 84.6 (2.8) | 94.0 (2.8) | 128.0 (3.1) | 163.8 (3.7) | 185.7 (3.8) | 203.5 (3.3) |
| Chemicals ........... | 51.0 (1.7) | 87.3 (2.9) | 120.4 (3.6) | 141.4 (3.4) | 168.0 (3.8) | 224.8 (4.6) | 246.1 (4.0) |
| Other ............... | 166.6 (5.5) | 176.6 (5.8) | 200.0 (5.9) | 257.2 (6.2) | 288.9 (6.6) | 310.7 (6.3) | 348.8 (5.6) |
| Total ............... | 508.1 (16.8) | 535.7 (17.6) | 620.9 (18.4) | 814.2 (19.7) | 887.9 (20.2) | 1,046.9 (21.4) | 1,263.7 (20.5) |

SOURCE: Department of Overseas Trade - Composition of Trade 1970/71 and 1972/73.
(p) Preliminary.

Table 2.14. VALUE ADDED AND EXPORTS OF MANUFACTURED GOODS BY MANUFACTURING INDUSTRY GROUPS 1968/69

| INDUSTRY GROUP | CONTRIBUTION TO MANUFACTURING VALUE ADDED % | EXPORTS AS % OF TOTAL MAN. EXPORTS | EXPORTS AS % OF TURNOVER |
|---|---|---|---|
| Food, beverages and tobacco | 16.6 | 33.4 | 9.9 |
| Textiles | 4.2 | 7.8 | 12.2 |
| Clothing and footwear | 5.2 | 0.5 | 1.0 |
| Wood, wood products and printing | 5.1 | 0.7 | 1.0 |
| Chemical, petroleum and coal products | 8.6 | 6.3 | 4.8 |
| Non-metallic mineral products | 5.2 | 1.9 | 2.7 |
| Basic metal products | 11.0 | 30.3 | 19.3 |
| Fabricated metal products | 7.8 | 2.6 | 2.4 |
| Transport equipment | 9.5 | 5.3 | 3.8 |
| Other machinery and equipment | 13.4 | 7.5 | 4.0 |
| Paper, paper products and printing | 8.2 | 1.2 | 1.1 |
| Miscellaneous manufacturing | 5.1 | 2.6 | 3.7 |
| Total manufacturing | 100.0 | 100.0 | 6.5. |

SOURCE: Adapted from data presented in Table 4.1.2 of the 1973/74 Industries Assistance Commission Annual Report.

Table 2.15. PERCENTAGE GROWTH IN EXPORTS OF MANUFACTURES 1963/64 - 1973/74

| | IRON AND STEEL % GROWTH | PETROLEUM % GROWTH | VEHICLES PARTS % GROWTH | MACHINERY % GROWTH | CHEMICALS % GROWTH | OTHER MANUF. % GROWTH | TOTAL MANUFACTURING % GROWTH |
|---|---|---|---|---|---|---|---|
| 1963/64 - 64/65 ...... | - 8 | -42 | 24 | 17 | 24 | 12 | 4 |
| 1964/65 - 65/66 ...... | 19 | -13 | 8 | 3 | 30 | 34 | 19 |
| 1965/66 - 66/67 ...... | 66 | 53 | 14 | 12 | 28 | - 1 | 20 |
| 1966/67 - 67/68 ...... | -18 | 10 | - 1 | 2 | 73 | - 2 | 3 |
| 1967/68 - 68/69 ...... | 13 | -21 | 27 | 8 | 39 | 18 | 18 |
| 1968/69 - 69/70 ...... | 26 | 5 | 69 | 35 | 17 | 28 | 29 |
| 1969/70 - 70/71 ...... | -33 | 50 | 9 | 33 | 18 | 17 | 10 |
| 1970/71 - 71/72 ...... | 17 | 45 | 23 | 18 | 35 | 6 | 19 |
| 1971/72 - 72/73 ...... | 53 | -24 | 45 | 8 | 9 | 11 | 17 |
| 1972/73 - 73/74 ...... | 15 | 128 | - 6 | 9 | 32 | 18 | 19 |
| Average Growth ...... | 15 | 19 | 21 | 15 | 31 | 14 | 16 |
| 1963/64 - 1973/74 .... | 190 | 169 | 490 | 269 | 1,235 | 253 | 332 |

Table 2.16. PERCENTAGE CHANGE IN EXPORTS OF CANNED AND PROCESSED MEAT 1968/69 - 1972/73

| TYPE OF MEAT | PERCENTAGE CHANGE | | | | |
|---|---|---|---|---|---|
| | 68/69-69/70 | 69/70-70/71 | 70/71-71/72 | 71/72-72/73 | 68/69-72/73 |
| Bacon, ham and other pigmeat ............. | 1 | 39 | - 2 | - 3 | 34 |
| Meat and edible offals n.e.s. .............. | 40 | 74 | 27 | 24 | 285 |
| Meat extracts and meat juices, fish extracts . | 53 | 85 | - 8 | - 8 | 140 |
| Sausages ............................... | 1 | 11 | 31 | - 7 | 37 |
| Other .................................. | 17 | 64 | 23 | -15 | |
| Total .................................. | 20 | 64 | 18 | -13 | 101 |

Table 2.17. AN INDEX OF VALUE OF SELECTED IMPORTS OF MERCHANDISE
(Base Year 1966/67 = 100)

| | FOOD BEVERAGES AND TOBACCO a) | CHEMICALS (INCL. PLASTICS) | TEXTILES, FABRICS, ETC. | METAL MANUFACTURES, MACHINERY, TRANSPORT EQUIPMENT |
|---|---|---|---|---|
| 1966/67 | 100 | 100 | 100 | 100 |
| 1967/68 | 99 | 109 | 107 | 111 |
| 1968/69 | 110 | 123 | 114 | 116 |
| 1969/70 | 116 | 132 | 122 | 127 |
| 1970/71 | 120 | 145 | 127 | 133 |
| 1971/72 | 124 | 139 | 133 | 113 |
| 1972/73 | 127 | 150 | 143 | 115 |
| 1972/73 | | | | |
| Dec. quarter | 134 | 142 | 138 | 113 |
| 1973/74 p) | | | | |
| Dec. quarter b) | 153 | 177 | 206 | 170 |

SOURCE: Australian Bureau of Statistics Exports and Imports of Merchandise at Constant Prices.

a) Food, beverages and tobacco includes meat, grains and vegetables (fresh), but can be taken as indicative of growth in manufactures in this sector.
b) Includes vessels and aircraft valued at $100.4 million at current prices.
p) Provisional.

Table 2.18. IMPORTS OF MERCHANDISE BY ECONOMIC CLASS
($000 f.o.b. port of shipment)

| PRODUCERS' MATERIALS FOR USE IN: | 1955/56 | | 1965/66 | | 1973/74 | |
|---|---|---|---|---|---|---|
| | $'000 | % | $'000 | % | $'000 | % |
| Building and construction | 61,608 | 3.8 | 93,600 | 3.2 | 253,372 | 4.2 |
| Rural industries | 13,200 | 0.8 | 40,360 | 1.4 | 70,599 | 1.2 |
| Manufacturing: | | | | | | |
| - motor vehicle assembly | 136,128 | 8.3 | 207,855 | 7.2 | 289,041 | 4.8 |
| - other | 615,960 | 37.6 | 1,015,816 | 35.0 | 2,027,175 | 33.6 |
| Total | 826,896 | 50.5 | 1,357,711 | 46.8 | 2,640,187 | 43.8 |
| Capital equipment | 355,176 | 21.7 | 838,533 | 28.9 | 1,536,855 | 25.5 |
| Finished consumer goods | 278,904 | 17.0 | 475,272 | 16.4 | 1,453,513 | 24.1 |
| Fuels and lubricants | 93,336 | 5.7 | 48,385 | 1.7 | 123,664 | 2.1 |
| Auxiliary aids to production | 56,568 | 3.5 | 92,471 | 3.2 | 119,569 | 2.0 |
| Munitions and war stores | 25,704 | 1.6 | 85,907 | 3.0 | 152,024 | 2.5 |
| Total imports | 1,636,584 | 100.0 | 2,898,280 | 100.0 | 6,025,814 | 100.0 |

SOURCE: Australian Bureau of Statistics - Overseas Trade Statistics Part 2 - Imports.

Table 5.1. INQUIRIES INITIATED MAINLY FOLLOWING SUGGESTIONS BY THE TARIFF BOARD OR THE INDUSTRIES ASSISTANCE COMMISSION SINCE 30/6/1967

| DATE OF REFERENCE | TITLE OF REFERENCE | DATE REPORT SIGNED | VALUE ADDED 1972-73 |
|---|---|---|---|
| | | | $ M |
| 21. 11. 67 | Mining, metallurgical, etc., machinery | 8. 2. 71 | -*[a)] |
| 21. 11. 67 | Steam engines, boilers and power units | 28. 5. 71 | -*[a)] |
| 30. 11. 67 | Engines, motors, pumps and valves, etc. | 7. 3. 72 | -*[a] |
| 19. 1. 68 | Drawing measuring and calculating instruments, etc. | 27. 6. 69 | 28.2[bc)] |
| 13. 3. 68 | Centrifuges | 10. 10. 69 | -*[d)] |
| 5. 6. 68 | Hand tools | 19. 11. 71 | 21.9 |
| 7. 6. 68 | Weighing machinery and weights | 29. 10. 69 | -*[a)] |
| 15. 7. 69 | Machine tools for working stone | 19. 7. 72 | -*[a)] |
| 20. 5. 71 | Domestic appliances, heating and cooling equipment, etc. | 10. 10. 73 | 244.7 |
| 20. 5. 71 | Agricultural machinery, etc. | 14. 6. 73[e)] | 72.6[f)] |
| 20. 5. 71 | Earthmoving, construction and materials handling equipment, etc. | 6. 8. 73 | 83.7 |
| 20. 5. 71 | Woodworking and Metal Working Machinery, etc.; gas welding etc. equipment and electrical welding etc. equipment, industrial and laboratory furnaces and ovens, etc. | 28. 6. 74 | 27.1 |
| 20. 5. 71 | Food processing machinery, etc. | 12. 6. 74 | 31.2 |
| 20. 5. 71 | Papermaking and printing machinery, etc. | 23. 7. 74 | -*[a)] |
| 20. 5. 71 | Textile and apparel making machinery | | |
| 29. 9. 71 | Lawn sprinklers; electric furnaces; electric welding, brazing and soldering machines, etc. | 14. 6. 73<br>28. 6. 74 [g)] | -*[h)] |
| 15. 6. 72 | Steam, gas and water fittings | 24. 5. 74 | 35.9 |
| 29. 8. 72 | Calcium carbide | 18. 4. 74 | -* |
| 6. 11. 72 | Tanned and finished leather; dressed fur | 24. 4. 75 | 20.7 |
| 6. 11. 72 | Leather and leather substitute products | 12. 6. 75[i)] | 24.8 |
| 6. 11. 72 | Hosiery | 13. 6. 75[i)] | 36.1 |
| 6. 11. 72 | Foundation garments | 28. 6. 74 | 23.6 |
| 6. 11. 72 | Primary shapes produced by rolling drawing, extruding of non-ferous metal | 12. 6. 75[j)] | 49.9 |
| 6. 11. 72 | Fibreboard containers, paper and textile bags | 23. 11. 73 | 119.1 |
| 6. 11. 72 | Miscellaneous industrial machinery | 27. 6. 75[i)] | 246.0[k)] |
| 6. 11. 72 | Pumps and Compressors | 5. 8. 75[i)] | 45.7[l)] |
| 7. 12. 72 | Colour television sets and components therefor | 27. 9. 73 | 435.6[n)] |
| 7. 12. 72 | Electric and electrical equipment | 27. 9. 73[m)] | |
| 23. 10. 73 | Clothing | 27. 5. 76[j)] | 399.3 |
| 23. 10. 73 | Headwear | 20. 6. 75[i)] | 3.9 |
| 13. 12. 73 | Mattresses, quilts, eiderdowns and cushions | 23. 8. 74 | 13.8 |
| 13. 12. 73 | Batteries | 15. 8. 75[i)] | 25.1 |
| 13. 12. 73 | Paints, varnishes and lacquers | 12. 8. 75[i)] | 73.9 |
| 13. 12. 73 | Steel pipes and tubes | | 150.9 |
| 13. 12. 73 | Cosmetic and toilet preparations | 30. 5. 75 | 61.6 |
| 24. 6. 74 | Pharmaceutical and veterinary products | 7. 11. 75[i)] | 140.8 |
| 24. 7. 74 | Measuring, checking precision instruments and apparatus, etc. clocks and watches, etc. | | -*[p] |
| 14. 8. 74 | Animal foods, etc. | 29. 10. 75[i)] | 53.4 |
| 30. 8. 74 | Agricultural tractors (bounty) | 12. 12. 75[i)] | -*[q)] |
| 20. 9. 74 | Railway and tramway locomotives, rolling stock, etc. | 23. 2. 76 | 144.7 |

Table 5.1. (continued)

| DATE OF REFERENCE | TITLE OF REFERENCE | DATE REPORT SIGNED | VALUE ADDED 1972-73 |
|---|---|---|---|
| | | | $ M |
| 14.11.74 | Acetyl products | 31.1.76 [r] | -* |
| 27.11.74 | Iron and steel | 28.5.76 [i] | 661.8 |
| Remaining inquiries in the Tariff Review program | | | |
| - | Jewellery and silverware | | 19.1 |
| - | Nuts, bolts, screws and rivets | | 39.4 |
| - | Metal cans and canisters | | 69.5 |
| - | Furniture | | 156.3 |
| - | Fabricated metal products | | 458.7 |
| - | Paper products | | 330.2 |
| - | Chemical products | | 79.8 |
| - | Miscellaneous manufacturing | | 14.3 |
| - | Sporting equipment | | 18.0 |
| - | Fabricated Steel structures | | 151.2 |
| - | Confectionary, chocolate and cocoa products | | 70.9 |
| - | Rubber products | | 47.3 |
| - | Miscellaneous Transport equipment | | 9.9 |
| - | Inks | | 13.4 |
| - | Brooms and brushes | | 13.7 |
| | Total | | $ 4,767.7 [m] |

Footnotes:

n.a. not applicable.
-* not available separately.
a) Included below - see footnote k.
b) Part only - see footnote n.
c) Also referred on 24.7.74.
d) Included below - see footnote l.
e) Includes part of reference dated 29.9.71.
f) Includes Agricultural tractors industry and industries in reference dated 29.9.71. Includes part of reference dated 29.9.71.
g) Included in reports on Agriculture machinery, etc., and Wood working and metal working machinery, etc., industries dated 14.6.73 and 28.6.74, respectively.
h) Included above - see footnote f.
i) Anticipated signing date.
j) Issued as a draft report.
k) Includes Mining, metallurgical, etc. machinery; Steam engines, boilers and power units; engines, motors, pumps and valves, etc. Weighing machinery and weights; machine tools for working stone; paper making and printing machinery, etc; textile and apparel making machinery industries.
l) Parts of this industry were also referred on 13.3.68.
m) Report on part of this industry issued as Consumer electronic equipment and components (27.9.73).
n) Includes parts of Drawing, measuring and calculating instruments, etc. industry.
o) No date set.
p) Also referred on 19.1.68 - see also footnote n.
q) Included above - see footnote f.
r) Included with proposed inquiry on Cellulose acetate flake.

Table 5.2. UNEMPLOYMENT STATISTICS

| MONTH | RETRENCHMENTS DUE TO STRUCTURAL CHANGE | | UNEMPLOYED PERSONS REGISTERED WITH CES |
|---|---|---|---|
| | NEW REGISTRATIONS WITH CES | AWAITING PLACEMENT | |
| July 1973 - January 1974 | 47 | 5 (January) | 121,082 (January) |
| February 1974 | 52 | 51 | 97,637 |
| March 1974 | 90 | 135 | 82,562 |
| April 1974 | 368 | 217 | 76,865 |
| May 1974 | 904 | 808 | 77,739 |
| June 1974 | 345 | 1,041 | 78,827 |
| July 1974 | 2,359 | 2,740 | 93,585 |
| August 1974 | 2,102 | 4,104 | 107,140 |
| September 1974 | 3,152 | 6,277 | 120,959 |
| October 1974 | 7,099 | 11,568 | 149,701 |
| November 1974 | 7,551 | 17,162 | 191,009 |
| December 1974 | 7,055 | 22,791 | 266,998 |
| January 1975 | 3,079 | 23,617 | 311,596 |
| February 1975 | 3,251 | 23,087 | 297,747 |
| March 1975 | 2,031 | 21,383 | 270,784 |
| April 1975 | 2,160 | 16,548 | 263,356 |

Table 5.3. ANALYSIS OF TARIFF PROTECTION OF MANUFACTURING INDUSTRY 1969/70

| CATEGORY | VALUE ADDED x) $'m | AS % OF TOTAL MANUFACTURING VALUE ADDED |
|---|---|---|
| Tariff protection available | 5,850 | 92 |
| a) value added in motor vehicles, machine tools and chemicals ........... | 471y) | 7 |
| b) value added when average effective rate is greater than 50% (including motor vehicles) ............... | 1,917 | 30 |
| Non-tariff related policies .... | 277 | 4 |
| No direct tariff protection or subsidy ..................... | 233 | 4 |
| Total Manufacturing ......... | 6,360 | 100 |

SOURCE: Based on figures contained in the Industries Assistance Commission Annual Report 1973/74, Appendix 3.4.

(x) Expressed in prices which would exist in the absence of assistance.

(y) Includes an amount relating to sulphate of ammonia, urea, cellulose acetate flake and sulphuric acid which has also been included in non-tariff related policies as it could not be separately estimated.

Table 6.1. SCHEMATIC DIAGRAM SHOWING THE MECHANISM OF GOVERNMENT IN THE FORMULATION OF POLICIES AFFECTING INDUSTRY

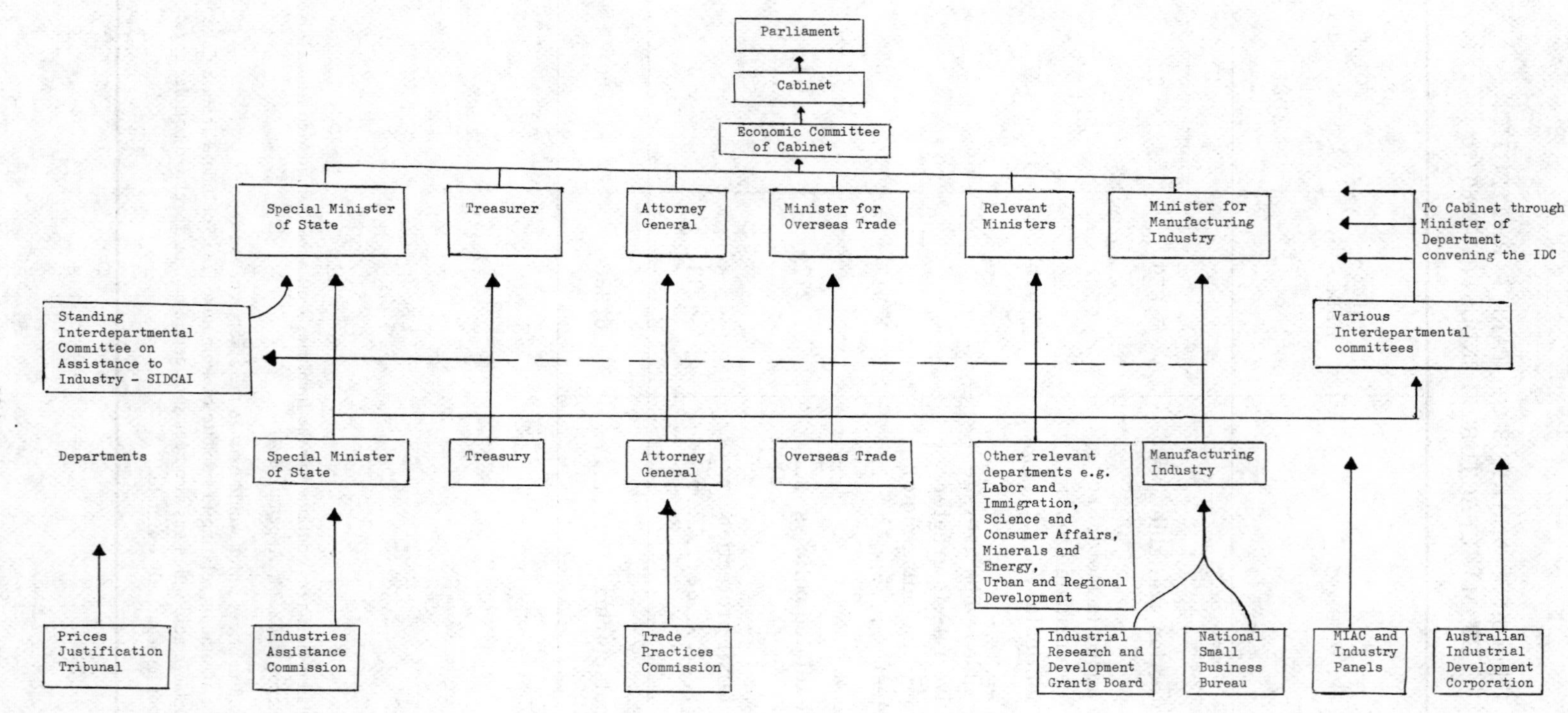


NOTE: Commissions and advisory bodies are usually responsible to the appropriate Minister (rather than the Department) although their reports etc in some cases are considered by the Department.

Table 6. 2. DEPARTMENT OF MANUFACTURING INDUSTRY

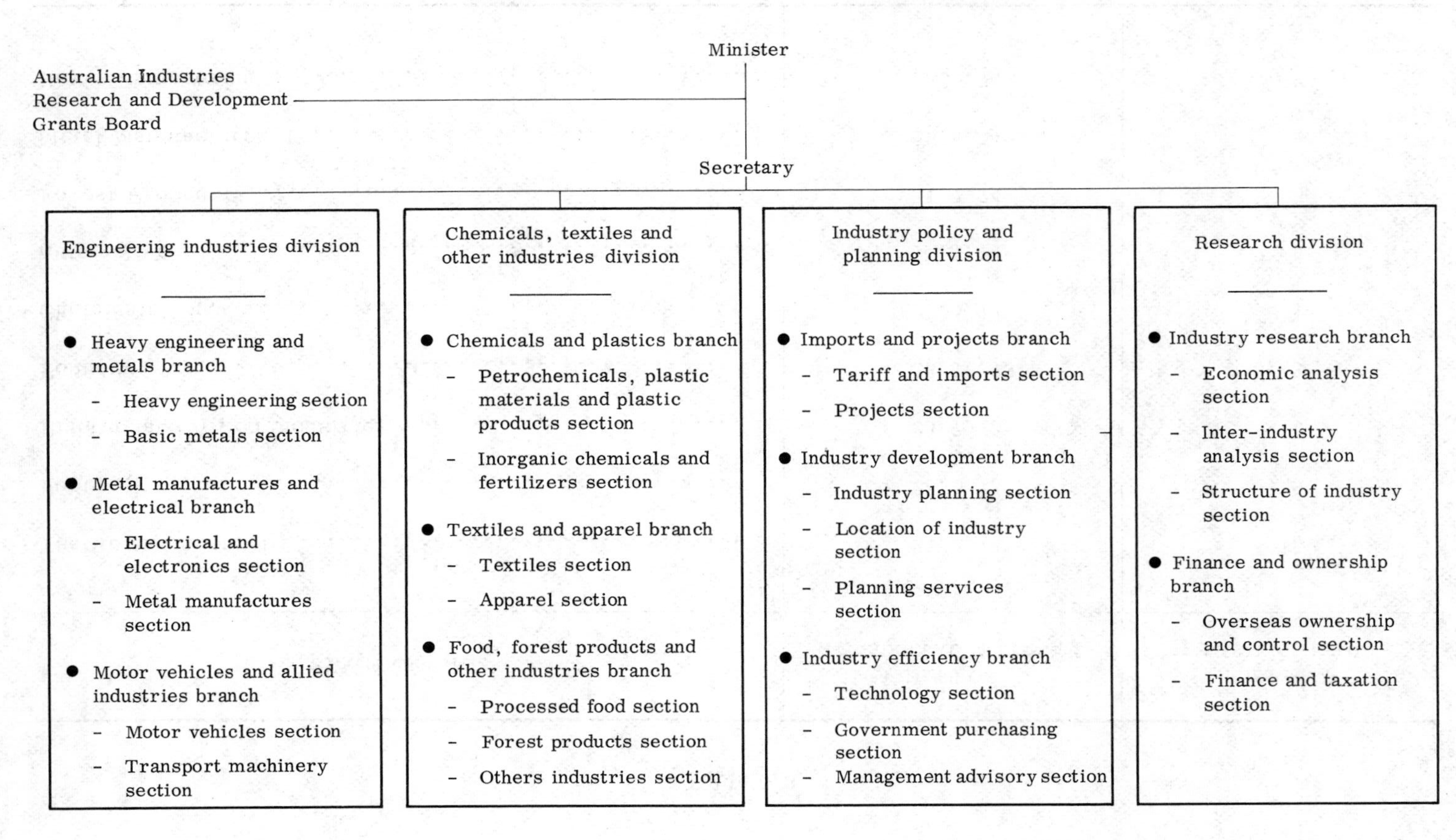

Table 6.3

| NAME OF PANEL | DATE OF INAUGURAL MEETING | NUMBER OF MEETINGS HELD |
|---|---|---|
| Textile and Apparel | 27.2.73 | 15 |
| Footwear | 28.5.73 | 9 |
| Printing and Allied Industries | 23.7.73 | 10 |
| Foundry | 23.10.73 | 3 |
| Chemicals | 26.4.73 | 4 |
| Automotive | 17.7.74 | 5 |
| Forest Products | 31.7.74 | 5 |
| Metal Manufactures | 29.8.74 | 5 |
| Heavy Engineering | 18.9.74 | 2 |

Table 6.4. MAJOR PROJECTS COMPLETED BY THE MANUFACTURING INDUSTRIES ADVISORY COUNCIL

Australian manufacturing industry in the next decade

Overseas investment in Australia

Taxation policy in relation to manufacturing industry

The tariff and national economic objectives

Growth of the national product

Major gaps in the Australian industrial structure

Investment allowances

Policy for secondary industry

Industrial research and development incentives

Restrictive trade practices

Pollution control

Submission to Jackson Committee

# ANNEXES

## LIST OF ANNEXES


| | | |
|---|---|---|
| Annex I : | "Foreign Investment in Australia", Prime Minister's address to the Australia-Japan Ministerial Committee meeting, Tokyo, 29th October, 1973. ........................ | 141 |
| Annex II : | "Foreign Equity in Mining", Prime Minister's guidelines for foreign equity participation in and control of the mining industry, 3rd November, 1974. ....................... | 144 |
| Annex III: | "Northern Territory Uranium"; statement by the Minister for Minerals and Energy, 31st October, 1974. ......................... | 147 |
| Annex IV: | "Structural Adjustment Assistance"; statement by the Prime Minister, 23rd April, 1974. ...... | 154 |
| Annex V : | "A Rational Approach to Tariff Reform"; speech by the Minister for Manufacturing Industry, 23rd May, 1975. ........................... | 158 |
| Annex VI: | "Conciliation and Arbitration in Australia" ..... | 169 |

## Annex I

# FOREIGN INVESTMENT IN AUSTRALIA

The following is the text of a statement on foreign investment in Australia, made by the Australian Prime Minister, Mr. Whitlam at the Australia-Japan Ministerial Committee Meeting in Tokyo on 29th October, 1973:

"The Australian Government recognizes that foreign investment in Australia is a matter of special significance for relations between our two countries. Australia is endowed with mineral resources of world importance. The proper development and prudent use of these resources is basic to our economic progress and growth. They are also of direct concern to you as a large and long term importer of raw materials. The policies that we pursue in the development of our natural resources and the nature of the partnership that is established between Australian and Japanese investment will be a major factor in the future of our two countries and of our region.

As you are aware the policy of my government is to adopt a more selective approach towards foreign investment in Australia than hitherto. No longer is there a wholly uncritical approach to foreign investment. We intend to ensure that foreign capital inflows are associated with productive investment which adds to Australia's real resources and brings us benefit.

This does not mean that we have no wish to see further overseas capital flow into Australia.

In the past foreign investment has made a very great contribution to the development of the Australian economy. Within a generation Australia has developed from a largely agricultural and pastoral economy into a modern, increasingly industrialized and diversified economy. The resources and know-how that the flow of overseas investment has brought have been of great value in this development.

We believe that overseas capital must continue to play a significant role, in partnership with Australian capital, in our future economic growth.

There is no general prohibition on foreign investment in Australia.

My government has the firm policy objective of promoting Australian control of Australian resources and industries. We also want to achieve the highest possible level of Australian ownership of our resources and industries. By the phrase "the highest possible level of Australian ownership" we mean the highest Australian equity that can be achieved in negotiations, project by project, that are fair and reasonable to both parties and are within the capacity of our own savings to support. However in some special energy case, which I shall mention shortly, we do have a particular objective of 100% Australian ownership.

There will be no discrimination against Japanese investment. Japanese investment will continue to be given treatment as favourable as that extended anywhere else.

This policy is being applied in a pragmatic way and all cases will be considered on their merits. This already applies in our examination of proposals under the Companies (Foreign Take-overs) Act. We aim to make our judgements taking into account the full circumstances of each new project or proposal, including such factors as the size and location of the proposed project, the use made of advanced technology, marketing arrangements, environmental aspects, labour relations and Aboriginal interests.

There are certain industries where we regard Australian ownership and control of particular importance. These relate especially to sources of energy where growing world shortages and other factors make this essential. Uranium is one of these energy sources and we have an objective of full Australian ownership in development projects involving uranium. We also regard this as a desirable objective in oil, natural gas and black coal.

We recognize however that Australia's resources of capital and technology are relatively limited, that the size of the projects to be undertaken is often very great and that we shall need to call upon overseas expertise, technology and capital to contribute to the proper development of these vital energy resources. Thus while we seek to require equity in new projects involving these four minerals to be in Australian hands, we do look for overseas participation in some ways: through access to technology, loans and especially long term contracts. The Australian Industry Development Corporation - AIDC - is a basic means by which the government will seek to ensure Australian equity and control and there are important areas in which AIDC will be able to work both with overseas companies and Australian investors. Proposed increases in the percentage of foreign equity in existing projects which already have high overseas equity may well be subject to particularly close scrutiny. Our general object is to moderate such holdings in these projects.

For other minerals our approach is more flexible. We desire partnership between Australian and foreign equity capital. I want to make it quite clear that there is no proscription of foreign equity participation in mining.

The nature of the partnership between Australian and foreign equity capital that is appropriate in each case will need to be assessed on its merits. In some circumstances it may be acceptable for foreign investors to participate significantly in decision-making in a project. The size of the project, the amounts involved, and the type of mineral are all factors to be taken into account. In pursuing our objectives we shall be flexible and guided by the practical needs of particular cases.

It is not our aim to have a different set of criteria for overseas participation in mineral exploration from those for participation in the development of proved mineral deposits.

In the uranium field in particular, and desirably also in oil, we aim to adopt the same sort of approach in exploration as I have already outlined for development of these minerals. However, in order to maintain a desirable level of exploration activity, we would, if necessary, accept a lower level of Australian ownership in exploration.

Given the limited Australian capital resources available and the higher risks usually involved in exploration, there is, however, much to be said for concentrating Australian equity at the production stage.

In some other sectors, successive governments have for decades restricted foreign investment. These include banking, civil aviation, radio and television and are no doubt well known to the Japanese government. Moreover investment from overseas for the establishment of new foreign-controlled life and general insurance companies is generally not favoured.

The government intends shortly to introduce legislation to control the activities of major non-bank financial institutions. Further overseas investment for the establishment of non-bank financial institutions is not favoured.

In relation to foreign investment in real estate, the Treasurer indicated in a statement issued on 20th March, 1973 that overseas interests should not enter into significant commitments for real estate purchases in Australia for the time being and that the Reserve Bank would not normally grant exchange control approvals for foreign investment in real estate. The policy on this matter, which relates to rural as well as urban land purchases, is under intensive study. In the meantime any specific proposals will be examined on their merits.

Let me emphasize however that in the generality of cases, for example in investment in manufacturing, our approach is a pragmatic one and that proposals by Japanese firms will be given equal weight to those by interests from other countries.

The Australian government believes that the policies on foreign investment, while designed to ensure a more selective approach than in the past, provide a framework which is flexible enough to allow mutually acceptable and beneficial arrangements through fair and reasonable negotiations. Our policies should establish relations between Japan and Australia on a sounder footing. If, there are any particular cases or questions that you have in mind, we would be happy to discuss them, either in the present meeting or subsequently."

Annex II

PRIME MINISTER

Press Statement No. 362

## FOREIGN EQUITY IN MINING

The Prime Minister, Mr. Whitlam, today released the guidelines agreed upon by the Government for foreign equity participation in and control of the mining industry in Australia.

Mr. Whitlam said the guidelines, which had been communicated to the Japanese Prime Minister, Mr. Tanaka, during his visit to Canberra, were a development of the policy outlined before the ministerial meetings between Australia and Japan in Tokyo last October. They were to be read in conjunction with the statement last week on the uranium industry by the Minister for minerals and energy, Mr. Connor.

3rd November, 1974

PRIME MINISTER

# GUIDELINES FOR FOREIGN EQUITY PARTICIPATION IN AND CONTROL OF THE MINING INDUSTRY

## 1. Development in Australian Interests

The Government's basic aim is to ensure that Australia's mineral resources are developed in such a way as to bring maximum benefits to the Australian people. If this objective is to be achieved, ultimate responsibility for the exploration, development and processing of minerals must rest with Australians: all enterprises, whether Australian or foreign-owned, engaged in exploration, development or processing, must conform with the national interest. The Government will use all of its powers, including its export and exchange control powers, to achieve this aim.

## 2. Equity, Control and Ownership

The Government desires, as a major objective, to promote Australian equity in and control of its resources and industries, and maximum Australian ownership compatible with Australia's long-term capital requirements and its needs for access to markets, advanced technology and know-how. The Government recognizes, however, that many of the important existing enterprises engaged in the development of Australian resources are under foreign equity control. For this reason, the promotion of Australian equity in and control of our resources and industries must be viewed as a longer-term objective.

## 3. Roles for the Public and Private Sectors

The Government recognizes that private participation in exploration and development will continue to be essential. A maximum level of activity will be achieved only if there is participation both by public bodies, such as the PMA and the AIDC, and private enterprises. The Government recognizes also that participation by companies will be dependent on the prospect of a return on capital employed which is commensurate with the high risks sometimes involved.

## 4. Exploration

The Government seeks Australian participation in mineral exploration. It believes, however, that because of the risks involved and Australia's limited capital resources, it is more important to secure a high degree of Australian equity participation at the production stage. The development of any mineral discoveries will, of course, be subject to approval by the Government in accordance with these guidelines.

5. Processing

The Government's objective is the maximum level of mineral processing consistent with the rational use of Australia's resources.

6. Consultations with the Australian Government

The Government expects to be informed of all major mineral development proposals - by Australian as well as foreign enterprises - at an early stage. The point of contact will be the Minister for Minerals and Energy who will refer to other Australian Government Ministers matters coming within their areas of responsibility - e. g. the Treasurer on foreign ownership and on financing aspects, the Minister for the Environment and Conservation on environmental aspects, and the Minister for Urban and Regional Development on urban and regional aspects. This will assist the Government in ensuring that maximum benefits accrue to the Australian people as a whole.

Annex III. 1

## NORTHERN TERRITORY URANIUM

Statement by the Hon. R. F. X. Connor, M. P.,
Minister for Minerals and Energy

My purpose in this statement is to outline the Government's programme for the rational development of uranium resources in the Northern Territory; a programme which will return substantial economic benefits to Australia from our supply of this vital energy resource to our overseas trading partners who face such grave difficulties in securing their energy requirements, and recognize fully the part played by those who have successfully explored our uranium resources.

Successive Australian Governments have recognized the economic and strategic importance of uranium. The first Australian legislation dealing with uranium and atomic energy was introduced by our predecessors in 1946. The 1946 legislation was amended in 1952 by the Menzies Government which in the following year introduced, with our support while in Opposition, an Act which now stands on the Statute Book as the Atomic Energy Act 1953-1973. The 1946 legislation declared that uranium and similar substances in the Northern Territory were the property of the Commonwealth; the Menzies legislation of 1953 confirms in Section 35 that these substances became the property of the Commonwealth on 11th September, 1946. The Menzies legislation also established the Australian Atomic Energy Commission with a range of functions extending to the exploration for, and mining, treatment and sale of, uranium and associated minerals. One of the Commission's first activities, as Agent of the Commonwealth, was, of course, to develop the Rum Jungle uranium deposit in the Northern Territory.

There are substantial reserves of uranium in the Northern Territory and I would remind the House that the first uranium discoveries in the South Alligator River area were made by the Bureau of Mineral Resources in 1953; Grievously, the information was not utilized by the then Government itself for the benefit of the people of Australia. And, too, the later discoveries of the Nabarlek and Ranger deposits were in areas recommended by the Bureau for uranium search in 1968.

The Annual Report of the Australian Atomic Energy Commission for 1973-74 states that reasonably assured resources in Australia are presently estimated at 188,000 tons of uranium forming a significant part of total estimated world resources which presently stand in excess of 1.6 million tons of uranium. Most of the Australian resources are located in the Alligator Rivers' Uranium Field of the Northern Territory.

That report also states that estimated cumulative requirements in the Western world in the period 1973 to 1990 are about 1.5 million tons of uranium and by the year 2000 a massive 4 million tons of uranium. The report published jointly last year by the International Atomic Energy Agency and the Nuclear Energy Agency of the OECD emphasized that new world resources of uranium for future requirements would have to be proven from the early 1980's. The United States of America, a country with substantial uranium resources of its own, seems now about to lift its embargo on imports of uranium in an endeavour to obtain adequate feed-stock for an expanded enrichment capability.

The knowledge of these emerging shortages has caused the large energy-consuming nations to scour the world for uranium supplies. This same knowledge has brought an end to the era of cheap uranium, a time in which I have been under much pressure inside Parliament, from the Opposition, and outside Parliament to approve give-away sales, e.g. proposed deliveries between 1977 and 1980 of 2,400 short tons of uranium oxide at prices of about $ A6.49/1b and, through the sale of 20% of the equity ownership in a major deposit to foreign interests, the delivery of 20% of the deposit at cost plus approximately 54 cents per lb.

In this context I need only mention the experience of the Tennessee Valley Authority, which in 1973 invited 53 uranium producers to tender for major supplies to it, and received offers, from only two and at a price for initial deliveries of about $ A9.24 per lb.

Major deposits of uranium have been discovered in the Northern Territory by the Peko Mines Ltd. and the Electrolytic Zinc Co. of Australasia Ltd. joint venture (the Ranger participants), Pancontinental Mining Ltd., Noranda Australia Ltd., and Queensland Mines Ltd. Despite the terms of the Atomic Energy Act, in last-minute decisions the McMahon Government approved export contracts for the sale of uranium to Japan by Peko/EZ and Queensland Mines at unsatisfactorily low prices.

Peko/EZ and Queensland Mines sought approval in the early months of our administration to sell to foreign interests part of the uranium deposits they had successfully explored - Ranger and Nabarlek. This, of course, flew in the face of the Government's policy on Australian ownership of uranium and other energy resources and was not approved.

All of this has strengthened our determination to bring order and coherence to the confusion that developed under the previous Government and to approach the development of this vital industry on a responsible basis.

Some countries have sought equity participation, albeit small, in the energy resources of other countries as a means of guaranteeing supplies from those resources. We have constantly assured our trading partners that this is not necessary and that we shall see that they receive supplies from our available exports. They understand our policy and appreciate our assurances of supply.

Whilst I have questioned the propriety of the approvals of uranium export contracts immediately prior to December 1972, I have stated on numerous occasions that this Government will ensure that the commitments under those contracts are met. But the Government has not been prepared to approve further export contracts because of the unsatisfactory nature of the market.

The Atomic Energy (Prescribed Substances) Regulations authorized me to issue under the Atomic Energy Act licences for the development of uranium deposits in the Northern Territory. After frustrating delays by the Senate Opposition, the Regulations were finally disallowed on 19th September, 1974 - a waste of six valuable months. Thus the Opposition in the Senate prevented my proceeding with licences for the companies which had successfully explored deposits in the Northern Territory.

Despite this frustration of the exploration companies by the Senate Opposition, the Government is determined to ensure that the Northern Territory uranium resources are developed in a sensible manner. Pursuant to the provisions of the Atomic Energy Act 1953-1973, the Australian Atomic Energy Commission will participate, as Agent of the Australian Government, in the mining and treatment, and undertake the sale, of the Government's uranium located in the Northern Territory and will also undertake all new exploration in the future for uranium in the Territory. I will now outline the Government's programme in more detail.

The Atomic Energy Commission will mine ore from the Ranger deposits, in conjunction with the Ranger participants, and at the appropriate time similarly from the other deposits. For the Nabarlek deposit, which is located within the Arnhem Land Aboriginal Reserve, the agreement of the Aboriginal people concerned must be given and their interests safeguarded before "mining" commences. These are matters within the administration of my colleague, the Minister for Aboriginal Affairs. For the Koongarra deposit the proposed Kakadu National Park must be declared and mining, when undertaken, must conform with the proposed legislation on National Parks and Wildlife Conservation. It is essential that the framework of a National Park be thoroughly established before uranium mining commences.

A uranium milling plant will be established in the Northern Territory financed by the Australian Atomic Energy Commission and the Ranger participants. It will have a capacity of 3,300 short tons of uranium oxide per annum and will be equivalent to that earlier proposed by the Ranger participants. It will treat ore from the Ranger deposits. The early duplication of the operation is envisaged.

My colleagues, the Prime Minister and the Deputy Prime Minister, and I have agreed with the Ranger participants in the terms attached on the construction and financing of the operation.

Future export sales of uranium will be negotiated by the Government within the special terms of Section 17 of the Act. Uranium oxide produced at the treatment plant will first be used to meet the existing approved contracts of Peko/EZ and Queensland Mines and the balance will be sold by the Australian Atomic Energy Commission as provided for by the Atomic Energy Act. It is anticipated that by the time of the commencement of the milling plant the market will be sufficiently mature for the negotiating of new export contracts. The approved contracts call for deliveries to Japanese power utilities commencing in 1977 but as uranium oxide will not be available from the treatment plant until some twelve months later, the Government will make available on appropriate terms and conditions, uranium oxide from its existing stockpile to ensure that each utility will receive the deliveries provided under the contracts. Uranium oxide produced following the re-commissioning of the Mary Kathleen mine could also be available for this purpose.

When Australia negotiates further sales it will do so as a willing seller seeking willing buyers. In particular, we will ensure that our major trading partners - Japan, Italy and West Germany - obtain an equitable share of the uranium we have for export. We will also take into account the Treaty on the Non-Proliferation of Nuclear Weapons. The Prime Minister, in his recent address to the United Nations General Assembly, stressed the importance of that Treaty and Australia, which has ratified the Treaty on the initiative of this Government, will naturally act with due regard to the obligations imposed by the Treaty and to the need to strengthen its application.

Our policy is to treat and fabricate Australia's minerals in Australia to the greatest practicable extent. The time necessary to bring the treatment plant into operation will enable full consideration of the technology to be used in a uranium enrichment plant to be built in Australia to upgrade the value of Australia's uranium exports. Existing enrichment technology is based on gaseous diffusion but considerable attention is being given to the centrifuge technology. To assist in our assessment of this technology the Australian Atomic Energy Commission was a member of the Association for Centrifuge Enrichment; this Association was formed in June 1973 by organisations from various countries, including Japan, to study all aspects to centrifuge technology. Last year we commenced discussions with the Japanese Government on collaboration in the establishment of a uranium enrichment plant in Australia including the joint acquisition of technology.

In its arrangements for the mining, treatment and sale of its uranium in the Northern Territory, the Government fully recognizes the exploration companies, some of which have a large number of small shareholders, which identified these resources. Their success will be rewarded. Between 1948 and 1961 rewards of up to $ 50,000 (aggregating to about $ 225,000) were paid to successful explorers for uranium in the Northern Territory, including the discoverer of the Rum Jungle deposit. The Government has therefore decided that a company which has undertaken successful exploration will receive the net proceeds from the sale by the Australian Atomic Energy Commission of 50% of the uranium oxide obtained from that deposit.

At today's estimated world price of $ A11 per lb. , 50% of the announced Ranger reserves, which total 110,000 short tons $U_3O_8$, have a gross value of $ 1,210 million and compared with some $ 714 million, when I was being pressed to agree to new sales contracts.

Because deposits explored by Queensland Mines, Noranda and Pancontinental will be developed later, the Government will consider separately the question of some earlier return for their shareholders.

Overseas countries are now exploring for uranium in Australia. in the expectation that successful exploration will carry with it a right, or entitlement, to a share of the uranium discovered. No special skills or technology are required for uranium exploration and the Government, as a matter of policy, does not wish to see foreign participation in new uranium exploration in the future. The amount of uranium to be exported to any country will not depend upon whether that country does, or does not, sponsor exploration for uranium in Australia. I have earlier referred to the criteria that will determine this matter. All new exploration in the future in the Northern Territory for uranium and kindred minerals will be carried out exclusively by the Australian Government through the Australian Atomic Energy Commission as provided in the Atomic Energy Act.

The Government's policies that I have outlined today are based on the recognition of the economic and strategic importance of uranium and of our obligations to the owners of the uranium - the Australian people - as well as to those members of the world community with limited access to energy resources. Australia is not alone in reviewing its policies on this important industry. I have already mentioned the review by the United States of America of its import embargo; Canada has recently announced changes in its policies designed to ensure that country receives a proper return from the development and utilization of its uranium resources.

31st October, 1974.

Annex III. 2.

## NORTHERN TERRITORY URANIUM

1. The title to Uranium in the Northern Territory is vested in the Australian Government pursuant to the Atomic Energy Act 1953-1973.

2. Regulations authorizing the Minister to issue licences for mining the uranium were disallowed by the Senate.

3. The Australian Government has therefore had to make different arrangements for mining the uranium through the Atomic Energy Commission pursuant to the Atomic Energy Act 1953-1973.

4. The mining of designated portions of the Ranger deposits, the delivery of the ore to a mill nearby and the construction and operation of the mill will be undertaken by Ranger Uranium Mines Pty Ltd. , of which half the directors will be nominated by Peko Mines Ltd. and the Electrolytic Zinc Company of Australasia Ltd. (hereinafter called the Ranger participants) and the other half by the Commission.

5. The mine and the mill and the necessary infrastructure will be financed by the Ranger participants and the Commission in the respective proportions of $27\frac{1}{2}\%$ and $72\frac{1}{2}\%$. The operation will have an initial capacity of not less than 3,300 short tons $U_3O_8$ per annum. The early duplication of the operation is envisaged.

6. Future sales of yellow cake produced at the mill will be negotiated by the Commission as agent for the Government.

7. The Ranger participants will provide their studies of future world markets for uranium and may introduce to the Commission particular sales proposals and the Commission will consult with the participants thereon.

8. The Ranger participants will receive the net proceeds from the sale of 50% of the yellow cake produced at the mill from ore mined in the Ranger deposits.

9. Deliveries to Japanese utilities pursuant to the export contracts of the Ranger participants approved prior to 2nd December, 1972 (or the repayment of borrowings of yellow cake undertaken for that purpose) will first be deducted from the Ranger participants' share of the yellow cake produced.

10. In calculating the net proceeds from the sale of yellow cake from the mill the proportionate costs of mining and selling and milling charges will be deducted from sales revenue.

11. The Ranger participants will be entitled to complete exploration within the terms of their existing exploration licences.

30th October, 1974.

Annex IV

PRIME MINISTER

Press Release No. 235
23rd April, 1974

## STRUCTURAL ADJUSTMENT ASSISTANCE

Cabinet today considered the policies to be pursued in future by the Australian Government in times of structural change. The details of the manpower program are currently being finalized by the Cochrane Committee, but the broad outlines of the ultimate scheme are clear. In the area of structural adjustment assistance to firms the Interdepartmental Committee has now reported and the Government has accepted their advice.

### Assistance to Individuals

In the case of employees affected by structural change a combination of income maintenance, retraining and re-location expenses are to be allowed for. As foreshadowed in the case of the 25% tariff cut procedures, displaced employees are to be paid an amount equal to their average weekly earnings for the previous six months - subject to a limit of $1\frac{1}{2}$ times average weekly earnings - for a period of up to six months. As an alternative there will be available, on a voluntary basis, an early retirement scheme. In addition, there will be a comprehensive retraining program designed to equip employees with relevant skills. During the training period generous income maintenance is to be provided. Details of the retraining and the removal aspects of the scheme must await the Cochrane Committee Report.

The scheme will be administered sufficiently flexibly for owners of small scale enterprises to be treated, if they so desire, as employees. Where it is possible, in terms of a simple set of criteria, for an employee to prove that he is unemployed as a result of a structural change induced by Government policy, these benefits will supersede the usual unemployment benefits.

The program will be administered flexibility and humanely by the Departments of Labour and Social Security. It will be of particular benefit to residents of country towns and to persons currently employed in declining industries.

## Assistance to Firms

Assistance to firms in the Secondary Industry area will be administered by a special Adjustment Assistance Agency responsible to the Minister for Secondary Industry.

Structural adjustment assistance is an innovation in industrial policy for Australia. The Government has decided to continually monitor the program at IDC level with a view to deciding whether the criteria for assistance decided upon today are adequate. In particular, the IDC will be charged with deciding, from time to time, whether structural adjustment due to Government initiatives should constitute the sole basis for justifying assistance.

The scheme will involve closure grants where relevant, consultancy grants to help firms adjust to changed circumstances when that is relevant, or loan guarantees.

## Criteria for Assistance to Firms

The criteria for eligibility for individual firms will be:

a) that the structural change had adversely affected, or was adversely affecting, the firm to the extent of rendering a significant separate part of its assets incapable of economic production; or that the desired change was unlikely to occur at a reasonable speed and at a reasonable economic cost without assistance to the firm; and

b) that the firm had taken reasonable steps for self-help, but that this was unlikely to enable complete adjustment by the firm (e. g. that the firm was unable to obtain finance on reasonable terms and conditions from normal commercial sources); and

c) that generally-available measures had been utilized to the full but were inadequate.

Consultancy grants for firms will be available on the basis of 50% consultancy cost to a maximum of $ 10,000.

Closure compensation payments to firms will be subject to the following conditions:

a) closure compensation to be paid in respect of the loss in value of fixed assets and stocks rendered unproductive by the structural change and incapable of economic use elsewhere in the firm or an associated firm;

b) claims for compensation to be within one year of the occurrence of the structural change;

c) payments to be on the basis of 85% of the difference between the written-down value of the assets for taxation purposes and their realized sales value.

Loan guarantees will be available to firms as a special measure and subject to the following conditions:

a) the provision of such guarantees to be covered by legislation;
b) the concurrence of the Treasurer to be obtained;
c) in relation to a particular line of activity loan guarantees to be subject to appropriate conditions and should not be available in addition to closure compensation.

This program will supersede all programs currently in existence.

Since coming to office, the Labor Government has been concerned to improve the allocation of resources in the Australian economy. It has sought to do this for two main reasons:

i) inefficient allocation of resources, especially if it is due to unduly high tariff levels, induces high cost industries to proliferate, with attendant injustices to consumers; and
ii) an economy built on an inappropriate structure, given its resource base and pattern of skills, adjusts to changes in the economic climate too sluggishly.

Good economic management in Australia will from time to time, therefore, dictate Government-inspired moves which will require resources to move from one use to another. We have seen this in the past year in the revaluations and tariff cuts announced by the Government. In future, there will be similar transfers of resources needed to accommodate the Government's urban, regional, defence and technological goals.

For sound economic and social reasons, the Government realizes a mechanism is needed both to promote and make easier the process of structural change. Worthwhile economic development will be more rapid if a scheme exists to promote, via various incentives, the resource flows needed to implement the desired changes. For a Labor Government, however, there is a more important point. If changes are desirable in the national interest, it is essential that the nation, not the individuals affected, should foot the bill.

Accordingly, in February 1973, the new Australian Government set in train two events. Under the leadership of the Department of Labor an expert group was set up to study the manpower programs essential to an efficient and humanitarian policy of economic change. Under the leadership of the Department of Secondary Industry, a working group was established to study the needs of industry in times of structural change. Both groups were charged with the task of evolving a set of policies which would make the process of change more efficient, combined with the requirement that the individuals affected by change in the national interest should not be required to suffer financially.

Some urgent structural changes could not wait on the deliberations of these two working groups. As a matter of principle, therefore, whenever during 1973 the Australian Government thought it necessary to initiate change - by way of revaluations or tariff cuts - it established generous, short-term specific adjustment programs. Notably in the case of the 25% tariff cut program, it was announced that the appropriate assistance measures were a prelude to a more general, permanent scheme.

A feature of the Government's Adjustment Assistance Program is that related to employers. The Government has already spelled out its general philosophy with respect to industry. Continuing assistance is to be provided only after detailed and public inquiry by the Industries Assistance Commission. Efficiency and enterprise is to be encouraged by a variety of measures, notable among which are the establishment of a National Management School at the University of New South Wales and the setting up of a Small Business Bureau. The former, based on a report commissioned by the previous Government but never acted upon, is designed to foster new management skills in Australia, while the latter is intended to assist businessmen in marshalling the resources available to them.

In the context of structural change the Government's new policies fit into the same philosophical framework. Emphasis is on encouraging the process of change, rather than simply compensating for loss of income.

Annex V

## "A RATIONAL APPROACH TO TARIFF REFORM"

Address by Senator, the Honourable James McCLELLAND
Minister for Manufacturing Industry
to
Harvard Club of Australia, Sydney, 23rd May, 1975

Since my election to the Ministry and my appointment to the portfolio of Manufacturing Industry, just three months ago, a great deal of my time has been caught up in dealing with the immediate problems presently confronting the manufacturing sector. Barely a day goes by without someone, some organisation - whether they represent the union or management side - coming to see me about fixing up some sort of problem. Therefore, in accepting your invitation to come along and speak to you tonight, I saw the opportunity of being able to "Come up for some fresh air"; to step back for a moment; to reflect; and to give you some of my thoughts as to where industry policy should be heading in the future.

I believe for reasons which will become apparent a little later on in my address that, at this point of time, it is especially important that we take a long hard look at where we are heading in the industry field in the longer term. I have deliberately chosen as my subject tonight the theme "A rational approach to tariff reform". I believe that this lies at the very heart of what we as a Government should be attempting to achieve in relation to the manufacturing sector.

Since assuming office two and half years ago the Australian Labor Government has endeavoured to use the tariff as an instrument to bring about a better allocation of resources in the manufacturing sector. We have tried to move in the desirable direction of achieving a manufacturing industry less reliant on the tariff than hitherto. These endeavours have, in general, represented a significant departure from past practices. It has, I might add, not been universally welcome by the manufacturing community, whether management or trade unions.

### Role of Tariffs in the Past

Traditionally, tariffs over the years have been used to build up industry; to encourage the replacement of imports with the local production of goods. This has occurred to a point where today we tend to have a very broadly based industry making a wide range of products with a domestic market orientation.

Under this philosophy tariffs have tended to become the principal instrument by which successive Australian Governments, of both political persuasions, have fostered the development of the manufacturing sector.

Tariffs have had a considerable influence on shaping the size and structure of the manufacturing sector. There has been a paucity of other specific policy instruments compared to our industrial counterparts overseas. Here I should mention that I draw a distinction between more general measures influencing overall economic development and those aimed specifically at the manufacturing sector. Indeed the term tariff policy has virtually been synonymous with what one might call "industry policy".

Under a policy of tariff protection Australia in the 1970's possesses an industrial structure which with some exceptions tends not to be primarily based on any sort of comparative or natural advantage. Rather its existence, at least in its present form and size, is dependent on the fact that it has been insulated to a degree from the international market place.

## New Orientations

As a Government we have generally taken a more critical look at the role tariffs should play in the development of the manufacturing sector. We have done this for two reasons.

Firstly, we believe that the circumstances or reasons which in the past gave rise to a general policy of high levels of tariffs are no longer as valid as they once undoubtedly were. For example, with the discovery, exploitation and export of our enormous mineral resources we do not have the same kinds of problems with the balance of payments that have plagued us in the past. In recent times there has been less concern to impose tariffs to develop industry to create employment opportunities for a workforce whose ranks were swollen by an in-flow of migrant workers. Defence considerations are also less relevant.

The second reason is that we believe the concept of import replacement as a basis for an industry policy offers only limited further opportunities for real growth, in absolute terms and in terms of increased productivity - both for the manufacturing sector and the nation as a whole. Whilst it might seem strange that a Labor Government is interested in the health of the private sector, the fact of the matter is that the achievement of the nation's social objectives and the raising of living standards demand that there should be an increased rate of growth in real income levels.

In this context the Australian Government believes that in the future the best prospects for growth must lie in those areas of production where Australia is, or should be, better suited. Therefore we believe industry should be encouraged to increasingly concentrate its development in those areas where we have a cost or natural advantage, or where at least our cost disabilities are least.

This will involve a movement of resources away from those activities which are relatively high cost, or highly protected by world standards, to those that fit in more with the kind of guidelines I have just mentioned.

Just as previous governments have looked to the tariff or other import restrictions as instruments in shaping industrial development in a certain direction, we too have attempted to use them to achieve progress in the different direction we have judged to be now appropriate. We have endeavoured to use downward changes in the tariff to provide the stimulus whereby the manufacturing sector is exposed to an increasing amount of international competition and thus induce a flow of resources away from those activities which need a high degree of tariff protection for their continued existence, to areas which require a lesser amount, or even none at all.

## General Approach

In the last two and a half years, for example, we took a number of major long term decisions to reduce the level and kind of tariff protection afforded a number of major industries.

We will continue to proceed with the progressive review of the tariff, which commenced just before we assumed office, and began by dealing with those tariff items which have relatively high levels of duty and have not been reviewed for many years. The review is a continuing one and will take some years to complete. The Government therefore has yet to take decisions on many of these cases. Whilst I do not propose to forecast what these may be in each case I believe that, as a general proposition, it would be desirable to look to a reduction in high rates of protection from imports. The maintenance of high rates of duty, except in the most exceptional circumstances, would be inconsistent with the general policy attitude which the Government has adopted to date.

In addition, the Government established the Industries Assistance Commission to replace the Tariff Board. It was created to develop amongst other things a more consistent approach towards the question of assistance not only for the manufacturing sector but also for other sectors of the economy as well.

That we want to make industry less reliant on the tariff in the industrial development process, and indeed place less reliance or emphasis on it as a tool or instrument of industrial policy, is illustrated by the action that was taken by the Government to reduce all tariffs by twenty five per cent across the board. The fact that this action was taken as an anti-inflation measure represented a departure from traditional thinking that tariffs were only altered for industrial development reasons.

The Government recognized that the reallocation process flowing from the lowering of tariffs could well cause hardships to both the employees and firms affected by the structural changes. So, for the first time in the context of Australian manufacturing industry specific measures aimed at facilitating the structural adjustment of industry were introduced. Following on the interim measures announced at the time of the 25% tariff cut the Government announced in April 1974 a permanent program of structural adjustment assistance whereby firms and employees could receive assistance if they were adversely affected by specified Government actions such as the decisions that we have taken to reduce the amount of long term tariff protection available to the consumer electronics and domestic appliances industries.

Under the scheme an employee is eligible to receive income maintenance payments for a period of six months, retraining and relocation assistance. For firms affected, they are eligible for consultancy grants, loan guarantees or if necessary closure compensation in respect of significant assets rendered uneconomic or incapable of use elsewhere in the firm.

In September 1974, we also introduced a program of Special Assistance to Non-Metropolitan Areas (known as the SANMA Scheme). We had always recognized that some country towns are heavily dependent on firms benefiting from a high level of tariff protection. The scheme provides for grants to firms to sustain or to enable an orderly phase-down in employment, for feasibility studies and for capital grants to assist in establishing alternative employment opportunities.

Setbacks

However, our moves towards achieving a more rational allocation of resources have I believe only been moderately successful.

In the beginning, during 1973 and most of 1974 I feel that there was probably some reason to believe we were achieving something meaningful. Changes were taking place but they were occurring at a manageable rate. In other words the economy was able to successfully accommodate these changes without too much disruption occurring. I believe that the combination of a buoyant economy and the structural adjustment programs that had been introduced, were probably adequately coping with the amount of change that was being brought about by our actions on the tariff front.

More recently, however, we have virtually been forced to halt the process, and in certain areas even to reverse it. Toward the end of 1974 the economy increasingly became unable to cope with the amount of change that was occurring in the manufacturing sector. This situation has been brought about by a combination of factors - principally the greatly increased level of imports that occurred, combined with a slackening in the general level of domestic economic activity. During 1974 imports rose in volume terms by some twenty eight per cent - compared to an average of only 2% for the other OECD countries.

In these circumstances we have had to resort to a number of emergency or short term measures in an attempt to slow down this rate of change and alleviate the disruption that has been occurring. In a number of sectors such as motor vehicles, footwear, textile and apparel products, domestic appliances, sheet steel as well as a number of others, we have acted to reduce the level of imports by imposing various import restraint measures. I might add that in addition there are a number of other requests for similar sorts of action from other sectors of industry. At this stage they are still in the pipeline. They have yet to come up for Government decision.

These actions, which have all been taken after consideration of advice from the appropriate body, e. g. the Textiles Authority or the Temporary Assistance Authority, are necessary if we are to stabilize the situation in the short run. I believe, however, their continuation for any protracted period will not be in the best interests of Australia. They will do nothing positive in the way of achieving a more rational allocation of resources and help to encourage the development of Australian industry better able to compete internationally. Once the immediacy of the situation has passed; once the factors that have given rise to these actions have changed, then the temporary restraints which have been imposed will have to be removed. In my own mind there is no doubt that this should happen.

I believe the great danger in imposing the import restraints that we have is that they may offer an inducement to firms and employees to move back into, or in extreme cases, to move into for the first time, those activities which we consider should have a lesser place in the future in the Australian industrial scene. If this did happen, if firms and employees were to move back, it would negate all that we have tried to do, all the pain that we have already gone through, over the last two and a half years.

Perhaps an even greater danger, and one that is of considerable concern to me as Minister for Manufacturing Industry, is that on a more general level firms and employees will believe that we are not really serious in our desire to continue with, to pursue, our long term objective of tariff reform. The motivation to preserve the status quo is, of course, always high. Governments are always subject to a high degree of political and social pressure to ensure that the status quo is maintained - or at least to make it very difficult for them to pursue a consistent policy of promoting change. If industry and employees do not believe we are serious as a Government then they will not be prepared to turn their minds to the very practical questions of making the right decisions about their future investment or their best long term employment prospects.

It is essential that if we are to succeed with a permanent program of tariff reform and industry restructuring in the longer term then we, as a Government, should, at this juncture, in this period where we have found it necessary to introduce temporary measures to allow a breathing space, reflect on the sorts of measures we need and the way we go about inducing structural change in the future.

## Some Basic Principles

Tonight I would like to briefly discuss the key elements which I consider to be necessary if we are to realistically achieve a permanent program of tariff reform. These might be broadly summarized as follows:

- a need to ensure that change occurs gradually;
- a need to ensure that adequate mechanisms exist to facilitate the adaptation process while it is underway;
- a need also to ensure that positive programs of an anticipatory nature are available where possible;
- a need to ensure that industry and the community generally are aware that we are serious in our intentions about tariff reform and
- a need to see that such a program takes place in an environment of confidence and understanding.

I would like now to briefly deal with each of these in turn. These are some lessons we have all learned and I will draw upon them. However, I do not pretend to have clearly in mind a firm and detailed program. Indeed, before coming to any firm conclusions I think we will all need to await the report of the Jackson Committee.

## A Philosophy of Gradual Change

One of the lessons we have learned is that change needs to be gradual. I strongly believe that to be otherwise is to invite disaster. If the rate of change brought about by a lowering of tariffs is greater than the adaptive capacity of the economy then it will result in too great an under-utilization of resources and too much social hardship. It will then be inevitable, and understandable, that both management and unions will bring pressure to bear to have tariff protection restored. It will mean that Governments will inevitably resort to the same sort of measures that we are resorting to at the present time.

We need to ensure that decisions which will induce structural adjustment in industry are taken in the light of an assessment of the degree to which the economy will be able to absorb or cope with these changes, within a reasonable time period. If the capacity is judged to be weak then the process must be slowed down or done in a different way. I might add that it is this kind of judgement that in large part determined the way in which we decided to facilitate long term structural change in the motor vehicle industry.

An essential prerequisite for a speedy program therefore is that the economy is reasonably strong and expanding and thus capable of providing quickly alternative opportunities for the resources displaced, either labour or capital. As a corollary the less strong the economy the greater the case for either delaying (for a time) the implementation of decisions resulting from the progressive review of the tariff, or a greater degree of Government involvement in the restructuring process. I should add that it is important however not be over cautious in assessing the resilience and initiative of private enterprise management and the capacity of the economy to absorb change.

A related, although somewhat different aspect, is that decisions to restructure individual tariff duties or reduce other means of assistance should not be seen as once and for all decisions. There is a need to continuously monitor the effects of individual decisions which induce restructuring, and indeed their progress, to determine either whether their combined effects have compounded to the stage where the rate of change is too quick within the manufacturing sector, or whether the program can be speeded up. In other words we must avoid the mistake of trying to do too much too soon as we have undoubtedly tried to do.

Within individual industries themselves we also need to ensure that the rate of change and progress, towards achieving a more desirable longer term structure, is not itself impeded by unnecessarily changing the conditions or parameters under which the industry operates too quickly. There can be a strong case I believe for phasing in reductions in tariff rates or other assistance for individual industries over a period of several years rather than introducing a once and for all drop in rates at one stage in time. This kind of phase-in period could be particularly applicable where a substantial reduction in the level of assistance has been recommended and accepted by Government. This kind of principle is not new. It has already been applied in the case of both the motor vehicle and shipbuilding industries.

There is certainly a clear need to avoid the sort of situation that occurred in the footwear industry where the reduction in tariffs by twenty five per cent across the board in July 1973 followed right on the heels of a planned program of tariff reductions for the industry to induce a measure of rationalization.

It must be clearly understood by industry however that a phased reduction is not a signal for a continuing guerilla war in an endeavour to get the Government to reverse its decisions, each time the next phased reduction is due to occur. Industry should be too busy with the constructive role of polishing and implementing its plans to cope with the adjustments that will be necessary. Of course there will be occasions when some delay or even an acceleration of the program will be warranted. This is a legitimate matter for debate and discussion with the Government.

## Structural Adaptation Policies

The second element that I mentioned as a necessary precondition for implementing a program of permanent tariff reform is the existence of an adequate and well developed program of structural adaptation assistance.

Recent experience has shown that the program which was introduced just twelve months ago has not been able to adequately handle the rate of change that has been occurring in the manufacturing sector. Obviously part of the problem has been due to the current economic situation. Another reason however could well be that the program being as new as it is; being barely twelve months old; lacking the experience which maturity will bring, is just not adequate to cope with the task with which it was confronted.

There is therefore a need, I believe, to develop and refine the scheme and to put it on a better administrative footing. We need flexible instruments that can be tuned to meet particular sets of circumstances - without of course their being so flexible as to be manipulated in ways inconsistent with their policy objectives.

There is I believe ample evidence overseas to suggest that industry restructuring will only occur against the backdrop of a well developed, well thought out structural adjustment program. I also believe there is adequate evidence here in Australia that the absence of such a program has in the past impeded the achievement of desirable structural reform.

It is important to bear in mind that by exposing the manufacturing sector to increased international competition we are imposing on industry a set of circumstances, to which it has to adapt, in addition to those that occur continuously - that go on almost unnoticed - such as changes in production technologies and consumption patterns. We need therefore to have well developed instruments available to help cope with this "additional burden" and we need them developed in advance as far as this can be done. This emphasis on anticipatory adjustment assistance measures and flexibility is in my view of critical importance.

In the absence of effective policy instruments there will always be a tendency on the part of Governments to fall back and use or adapt those instruments which it does have available. One need only reflect on the way in which adaptation problems in industry were dealt with in the early 1960's when industry was exposed to increased international competition with the removal of import licensing to see this point. As the only mechanism then available tariffs were increasingly and inevitably used to overcome these problems.

## Anticipatory Programs

In the context of pursuing a policy of tariff reform and of placing lesser reliance on the tariff as an instrument of development policy we need to ensure that the future direction and pace of industrial development is not impeded by any omission on the Government's part to provide adequate support and guidance where this is considered necessary.

While our present structural adaptation policies are aimed at facilitating the movement of resources they are at present essentially negative in character in that they tend only to "pick up the pieces". There is I believe a need to look at the other side of the coin; to examine what positive or anticipatory measures are needed to reinforce and complement the moves we take on the tariff front. We need to ensure that in our drive to achieve a better industrial structure the resources released from so called "high cost" areas of production can be fully utilized and utilized in the most productive way possible.

We do, of course, already have a number of what might be called positive instruments. The Industrial Research and Development Grants Scheme and the National Small Business Bureau, are cases in point. It would seem that if the program of tariff reform is to be successfully implemented then we need to critically examine the adequacy of these specific programs for they will tend to assume a much greater importance in the future in helping the private sector to adjust to, anticipate and even foster desirable change.

As importantly, a sustained period of structural adjustment is likely to lead to changes in the size and kind of demands for finance which the manufacturing sector will place upon the financial community. If the pattern of our industrial structure is to be altered significantly then the demand for risk capital is likely to increase. This has significant implications for the financial sector, which has developed in the post war period in a different environment. It also could have implications for the way in which Governments treat company taxation. In brief, the policies and practices of both Governments and other sectors of the economy which relate to the manufacturing sector must become attuned positively to the different direction in which our industry structure is now heading. If they do not then the structural adaptation process will be delayed or impeded to the nation's loss.

Serious Intentions

The fourth point I mentioned in relation to tariff reform was the need to make the manufacturing community aware that we are serious in our desire to achieve a more rational allocation of resources. Essentially this involves untying the straightjacket in which everyone's thinking tends to resolve around the belief that the solution to industry problems is brought about by an upward manipulation of the tariff. This kind of thinking inevitably involves a rush on the tariff making machinery every time a problem arises.

A permanent program of tariff reform involves the manufacturing sector continuously adapting, with the assistance of positive Government instruments where this is considered necessary, around a long term tariff rate. As I have said there is a need to ensure that the positive adaptation instruments are adequately developed and available to be called on when required so that there will not be a need or at least be a lesser need, to ressort to the tariff.

However this may not be enough. I have heard it said for example that as long as industry believes that there is ready recourse to the Temporary Assistance Authority then they will not accept that the Government is serious as to its intentions. I, for one, can see that this is a reasonable stance for industry to take.

One of the areas we therefore need to take a hard look at is whether the present way we go about setting long term tariff rates is really helping us as a nation to achieve permanent tariff reform. Perhaps there could be other ways. Perhaps we should consider, if in practice the end result is to be a broad banding of the tariff at reasonably low levels whether we could get to this point in ways which facilitate the adaption by industry more easily. I have the feeling in my bones, perhaps quite wrongly, that there is an issue here which needs airing. I would hope that the Jackson Committee in its report will address itself to this kind of issues.

## Confidence and Understanding

The implementation of a policy of tariff reform needs to take place within an environment of business and community confidence. I have already indicated that one of the necessary pre-conditions for promoting structural change is a healthy economy capable of providing alternative opportunities for displaced resources.

The present economic situation is such that it hardly helps in this regard. However one of the things that seems clear to me is that without adequate Government, industry and community consultative mechanisms then the task of obtaining better understanding of the issues and problems surrounding industry policy and development will be that much harder. We have made a start with the industry panel system but more needs to be done.

The fact that we have endeavoured to improve both the internal and external competitive environment has led, in part, to the Government being labelled as "business bashers". This is unfortunate for as I said earlier, and the Prime Minister made a similar point in a recent speech to the Sydney Chamber of Commerce, the health of the private sector is of intimate concern to us for it ultimately affects the health of the whole community.

Improved communication between Government and the private sector is I believe one answer. Government, I think, needs to explain its policies in a clearer, more precise way. Business on the other hand needs to put its needs to Government in a way that they can clearly be seen to be compatible with the long term national interest. There just has to be a better understanding reached between business and Government than there exists at present.

I might mention in this context that I sometimes believe that I have a greater faith in the private sector's capacity (at least in manufacturing industry) to meet the challenges of the future than do many businessmen. I regularly hear expressions of concern about socialization and Government interference, and wild talk about destruction of the private enterprise system. Yet many of these same intelligent alert and responsible businessmen, when asked what they wish the Government to do, respond by asking for Government financial or tariff assistance. It is just not on, and never has been, to ask for Government assistance to be given or maintained, and yet not expect that a degree of Government involvement in the industry will follow.

I firmly believe that Government involvement in industry should be at a minimum. I also firmly believe that if Government assistance is given - and I include tariff protection here - then the Government has a responsibility to ensure that it is utilized in the direction of facilitating the national interest. After all, this is the reason it was, or should be, given in the first place.

## Conclusion

Mr. President, I have endeavoured to reflect this evening on what might be the necessary ingredients to successfully implement a permanent program of tariff reform. As I said earlier, I do not pretend to have all the answers at this stage. We will however all be in a better position, I believe, after we have had the benefit of digesting the Jackson Committee report which I understand should be available shortly. In the meantime I hope that what I have said tonight has provided some food for thought about one of the key issues of economic and social policy presently facing us in Australia. If we do not solve the problem of advancing a rational approach to tariff reform then our economic problems will become greater and opportunities for successful industrial development will have been lost - perhaps forever.

Annex VI

## CONCILIATION AND ARBITRATION IN AUSTRALIA

### Introduction

The basis of Federal industrial regulation in Australia is a system of conciliation and arbitration developed to prevent and settle industrial disputes. This system is built on the proposition that when employers and employees are unable to reach agreement on an industrial matter through negotiation the law should provide a means for resolving the matter by independent conciliation and, if conciliation fails, by arbitration.

### The Objects of the Conciliation and Arbitration Act

The chief objects of the Conciliation and Arbitration Act are as follows:

a) to promote goodwill in industry;
b) to encourage and provide means for conciliation with a view to amicable agreement, thereby preventing and settling industrial disputes;
c) to provide means for preventing and settling industrial disputes not resolved by amicable agreement, including threatened, impending and probable industrial disputes, with the maximum of expedition and the minimum of legal form and technicality;
d) to provide for the observance and enforcement of agreements and awards made for the prevention or settlement of industrial disputes;
e) to encourage the organisation of representative bodies of employers and employees and their registration under this Act; and
f) to encourage the democratic control of organisations so registered and the full participation by members of such an organisation in the affairs of the organisation.

Although the Act is one of the most amended Federal statutes the substance of the objects has remained by and large the same since 1904.

### The Australian Conciliation and Arbitration Commission

The Commission consists of a President, Deputy Presidents and Commissioners. At July, 1974 the Commission comprised the President, nine Deputy Presidents and nineteen Commissioners. The

President and the Deputy Presidents, who are referred to as presidential members, have the status of a judge, but retire from office at the age of 65 or at the age of 70 if appointed prior to 1972. To be appointed as a presidential member a person must be a barrister or solicitor of not less than five years' standing or, except for appointment as the President, have a high level of experience in industry, commerce, industrial relations, government, or must have held certain academic qualifications for at least five years. No statutory qualifications are prescribed for Commissioners. However, they are usually men of proven status, experience and ability in the industrial field and are drawn from the ranks of unions, employer organisations or government.

The Commission is the institution which carries out the functions of conciliation and arbitration. In general, the Commissioners are responsible for the day-to-day work of resolving disputes and the making of awards, while the presidential members deal with the more important matters which have either been referred from Commissioners or specially allocated to them by the President or by operation of the Act itself.

The Act prescribes that certain matters must be dealt with by a "Full Bench", this being of at least three members of the Commission, two of whom must be presidential members, and all of whom are nominated by the President.

These matters include making provision for or altering wage rates on grounds predominantly related to the national economy and without examination of the work or industry in which the persons are employed, a minimum wage for adults and for standard hours of work, annual leave and long service leave.

In addition the President, on the request of any party to a dispute, can determine that a matter should "in the public interest" be dealt with by a Full Bench. A Full Bench can also hear an appeal against a decision of a member of the Commission if it decides the matter is of such importance that it is in the public interest to do so.

The President is the head of the Commission and assigns particular industries or groups of industries to panels of Commissioners, each under the guidance of a presidential member who allocates work in respect of these industries to members of that panel. The President may assign a Deputy President and, subject to any directions of that Deputy President, a Commissioner to deal with industrial questions in certain industries (e. g. the maritime and stevedoring industries) in relation to which the Australian Parliament has special powers under the Constitution.

The co-ordination of the work of the Commission is aided by conferences which the President is required to summon at least once a year to enable all members of the Commission to discuss matters relating to their functions, and particularly "means for ensuring expedition in the settlement of industrial disputes". Once a year, the

President is required to furnish a report on the work of the Commission and on the extent to which the objects of the Act have been achieved. This report is to the Minister for Labor and Immigration and is presented to the Parliament.

# BIBLIOGRAPHY

## A. AUSTRALIAN PUBLICATIONS


### Academic Publications

Arndt, H. W. and Boxer, A. H. , "The Australian Economy", Cheshire, 1972.

Boehm, E. A. "20th Century Economic Development in Australia". Longman, 1970.

Davidson, F. G. "The Industrialization of Australia". MUP, 1969.

Downing, R. I. (ed. ) "The Australian Economy - a manual of applied economics". Weidenfeld and Nicolson, London, 1973.

Forster, C. (ed. ) "Australian Economic Development in the Twentieth Century". ANU, 1970.

Shaw, A. G. L. "The Economic Development of Australia". Longman, 1970.

Melbourne Institute of Applied Economic and Social Research "Autralian Economic Review". MUP Quarterly.

### Committee Reports

"Report of the Committee of Economic Enquiry" ("Vernon Report"), 1965.

"Review of the Continuing Expenditure Policies of the Previous Government (Coombs Task Force) Report", 1973.

"Report of the Committee to Review Government Procurement Policy" (Scott Committee). April 1975.

"Taxation Review Committee (Asprey Committee) Interim Report", September 1974 (final report released May 1975).

"Report of Committee of Inquiry into Inflation and Taxation", May 1975.

### Consultant's Publications

International Technical Services "Study of the Rate of Diffusion of New Technology", Office of Secondary Industry, 1972.

### Departmental Publications

#### Australian Bureau of Statistics

"Census of Manufacturing Establishments" 1972/73 (Preliminary Statement).

"Manufacturing Establishments - Details of Operations by Industry Class, Australia" 1968/69.

"Industry Concentration Statistics" 1968/69.
"Exports and Imports of Merchandise at Constant Prices".
"Overseas Trade Statistics, Part 2, Imports" 1974.

Industries Assistance Commission

"Annual Report" 1973/74.
Specific industry reports, and in particular -
Report on "Passenger Motor Vehicles" July, 1974.

Department of Manufacturing Industry

"R and D in Manufacturing Industry 1971-72", November 1974.
"Developments in Manufacturing Industry" Quarterly.
"Survey of Manufacturing Activity" Quarterly.
"Income Tax for the Manufacturer", Office of Secondary Industry, 1971.

Department of Overseas Trade

"Composition of Trade" 1970-71 and 1972-73.

Tariff Board Reports

Annual Reports 1970-71 and 1972-73.
Specific industry reports and in particular:
- Agricultural Tractors, 2/9/66 and 21/12/72.
- Chemical Industry - Support Values Review, 29/4/68.
- Consumer Electronic Equipment and Components, 27/9/73.
- Domestic Appliances, Heating and Cooling Equipment, etc., 10/10/73.
- Footwear, 12/8/66.
- Footwear with Non-Leather Uppers, 8/4/70.
- Industrial Chemicals and Synthetic Resins, 13/4/66 and 10/12/71.
- Knitted Shirts and Outer Garments, 29/4/71.
- Metal Working Machine Tools and Accessories, 14/4/72.
- Products of the Printing Industry, 21/9/73.
- Woven Shirts, etc., 6/5/71.

Temporary Assistance Authority Reports

Certain Consumer Electronic Equipment and Components, 17/3/75.
Certain Plastic Products, 4/4/75.
Chain Saws, 11/3/75.
Colour Television Receivers with a Screen Size not less than 47 cm., 17/3/75.
Fine Paper, 11/3/75.
Footwear and Parts therefor, 10/10/74.
Injection Moulding Machines, 23/12/74.
Precision Ground Steel Ball Bearings, 4/3/75.
Refrigerators, Washing Machines and Rotary Clothes Dryers, 22/2/75.
Steel Sheet and Coil, 12/2/75.
Tyres (Motor Vehicles), 2/1/75.

Textile Authority Reports

Apparel (Knitwear and Other Items of), 21/4/75.
Apparel - Section 1 (Men's Shirts, Woven Pyjamas and other Woven Nightwear), 24/12/74.
Certain Items of Apparel, 5/7/74.
Certain Textile Floorcoverings, 7/2/75.
Certain Yarns and Textile Products, 30/4/75.
Polyolefin Bags and Sacks, 29/3/75.
Yarns and Textile Products, 10/11/74.

Department of the Treasury

Treasury Information Bulletin (quarterly).

Government Legislation

"Australian Industries Development Corporation Act 1975".
"Industries Assistance Commission Act 1973".
"Industrial Research and Development Grants Act 1967" and amendments 1972 and 1973.
"Export Finance and Insurance Corporation Act 1974".
"Export Market Development Grants Act 1974".
"The Financial Corporation Act 1974".

Government Policy Statements

"Australian Labor Party Policy" Speech by Hon. E. G. Whitlam, 1972.
"Australian Labor Party Policy" Speech by Hon. E. G. Whitlam, 1974.
"ALP 29th Commonwealth Conference" Launceston 1971 Relevant Papers.
"ALP 30th Federal Conference" Surfers Paradise 1973 Relevant Papers.

International Organisations

"UN Monthly Bulletin of Statistics", July 1974.
"OECD Economic Surveys - Australia", December 1972.

Press Releases

"Green Paper on Manufacturing Industry", Prime Minister, 18/7/74.
"New Assistance Arrangements for Australian Shipbuilding Industry", Minister for Secondary Industry and Minister for Supply, 18/12/73.
"Reduction of Sales Tax on Passenger Motor Vehicles", Treasurer, 28/1/75.
"Regional Employment Development Scheme", Minister for Labor and Immigration, 11/9/74.
"Special Assistance to Non-metropolitan Areas" (SANMA), Prime Minister, 22/10/74.
"Structural Adjustment Assistance", Prime Minister, 23/4/74.

"Tariff Review", Minister for Trade and Industry, 15/3/71.
"Visiting Industrial Experts Grants Scheme", Acting Minister for Secondary Industry, 14/5/73.

Speeches

"Budget Speech 1973/74", House of Representatives Hansard, 21/8/73, pp. 32-165.
"Budget Speech 1974/75", House of Representatives Hansard, 17/9/74, pp. 1275-1425.
"Productivity through Technology", Minister for Labor and Immigration, 24/8/73.
"Second Reading Speech on Industries Assistance Commission Bill" House of Representatives Hansard, 27/9/73, pp. 1631-1635.
"Tabling Speech on Industries Assistance Commission First Annual Report", Prime Minister, 29/10. 74.
"Foreign Investment in Australia" Prime Minister's speech to Australia - Japan Ministerial Committee meeting. Tokyo, 29th October 1973.
"Foreign Equity in Mining", Prime Minister. 3rd November 1974.
"Northern Territory Uranium", Minister for Minerals and Energy, 31st October 1974.
"A Rational Approach to Tariff Reform" Minister for Manufacturing Industry, 23rd May 1975.

Trade Agreements

"UK/Australia Trade Agreement" 1932.

Additional Reading

"Export Market Development Grants - a guide to available benefits", Export Development Grants Board, 1975.
"Overseas Investment Insurance", Export Finance and Insurance Corporation.
"Capital Goods", Export Finance and Insurance Corporation.
"Comprehensive Policies", Export Finance and Insurance Corporation.
"Supplementary Facilities", Export Finance and Insurance Corporation.

## B. OECD PUBLICATIONS ON INDUSTRIAL POLICY

"United States Industrial Policies", OECD, 1970.
"The Industrial Policy of Austria", OECD, 1971.
"The Industrial Policies of 14 Member Countries", OECD, 1971.
"The Industrial Policy of Japan", OECD, 1972.
"The Industrial Policy of France, OECD, 1974.
"The Aims and Instruments of Industrial Policy: A Comparative Study", OECD, 1975.

# OECD SALES AGENTS
# DEPOSITAIRES DES PUBLICATIONS DE L'OCDE

**ARGENTINA – ARGENTINE**
Carlos Hirsch S.R.L.,
Florida 165, BUENOS-AIRES.
☎ 33-1787-2391 Y 30-7122

**AUSTRALIA – AUSTRALIE**
International B.C.N. Library Suppliers Pty Ltd.,
161 Sturt St., South MELBOURNE, Vic. 3205.
☎ 69.7601
658 Pittwater Road, BROOKVALE NSW 2100.
☎ 938 2267

**AUSTRIA – AUTRICHE**
Gerold and Co., Graben 31, WIEN 1.
☎ 52.22.35

**BELGIUM – BELGIQUE**
Librairie des Sciences
Coudenberg 76-78, B 1000 BRUXELLES 1.
☎ 512-05-60

**BRAZIL – BRESIL**
Mestre Jou S.A., Rua Guaipá 518,
Caixa Postal 24090, 05089 SAO PAULO 10.
☎ 256-2746/262-1609
Rua Senador Dantas 19 s/205-6, RIO DE JANEIRO GB. ☎ 232-07. 32

**CANADA**
Information Canada
171 Slater, OTTAWA. KIA 0S9.
☎ (613) 992-9738

**DENMARK – DANEMARK**
Munksgaards Boghandel
Nørregade 6, 1165 KØBENHAVN K.
☎ (01) 12 69 70

**FINLAND – FINLANDE**
Akateeminen Kirjakauppa
Keskuskatu 1, 00100 HELSINKI 10. ☎ 625.901

**FRANCE**
Bureau des Publications de l'OCDE
2 rue André-Pascal, 75775 PARIS CEDEX 16.
☎ 524.81.67
Principaux correspondants :
13602 AIX-EN-PROVENCE : Librairie de l'Université. ☎ 26.18.08
38000 GRENOBLE : B. Arthaud. ☎ 87.25.11
31000 TOULOUSE : Privat. ☎ 21.09.26

**GERMANY – ALLEMAGNE**
Verlag Weltarchiv G.m.b.H.
D 2000 HAMBURG 36, Neuer Jungfernstieg 21
☎ 040-35-62-500

**GREECE – GRECE**
Librairie Kauffmann, 28 rue du Stade,
ATHENES 132. ☎ 322.21.60

**HONG-KONG**
Government Information Services,
Sales of Publications Office,
1A Garden Road,
☎ H-252281-4

**ICELAND – ISLANDE**
Snaebjörn Jónsson and Co., h.f.,
Hafnarstræti 4 and 9, P.O.B. 1131,
REYKJAVIK. ☎ 13133/14281/11936

**INDIA – INDE**
Oxford Book and Stationery Co. :
NEW DELHI, Scindia House. ☎ 47388
CALCUTTA, 17 Park Street. ☎ 24083

**IRELAND – IRLANDE**
Eason and Son, 40 Lower O'Connell Street,
P.O.B. 42, DUBLIN 1. ☎ 01-41161

**ISRAEL**
Emanuel Brown :
35 Allenby Road, TEL AVIV. ☎ 51049/54082
also at :
9, Shlomzion Hamalka Street, JERUSALEM.
☎ 234807
48 Nahlath Benjamin Street, TEL AVIV.
☎ 53276

**ITALY – ITALIE**
Libreria Commissionaria Sansoni :
Via Lamarmora 45, 50121 FIRENZE. ☎ 579751
Via Bartolini 29, 20155 MILANO. ☎ 365083
Sous-dépositaires :
Editrice e Libreria Herder,
Piazza Montecitorio 120, 00186 ROMA.
☎ 674628
Libreria Hoepli, Via Hoepli 5, 20121 MILANO.
☎ 865446
Libreria Lattes, Via Garibaldi 3, 10122 TORINO.
☎ 519274
La diffusione delle edizioni OCDE è inoltre assicurata dalle migliori librerie nelle città più importanti.

**JAPAN – JAPON**
OECD Publications Centre,
Akasaka Park Building,
2-3-4 Akasaka,
Minato-ku
TOKYO 107. ☎ 586-2016
Maruzen Company Ltd.,
6 Tori-Nichome Nihonbashi, TOKYO 103,
P.O.B. 5050, Tokyo International 100-31.
☎ 272-7211

**LEBANON – LIBAN**
Documenta Scientifica/Redico
Edison Building, Bliss Street,
P.O.Box 5641, BEIRUT. ☎ 354429 – 344425

**THE NETHERLANDS – PAYS-BAS**
W.P. Van Stockum
Buitenhof 36, DEN HAAG. ☎ 070-65.68.08

**NEW ZEALAND – NOUVELLE-ZELANDE**
The Publications Officer
Government Printing Office
Mulgrave Street (Private Bag)
WELLINGTON, ☎ 46.807
and Government Bookshops at
AUCKLAND (P.O.B. 5344). ☎ 32.919
CHRISTCHURCH (P.O.B. 1721). ☎ 50.331
HAMILTON (P.O.B. 857). ☎ 80.103
DUNEDIN (P.O.B. 1104). ☎ 78.294

**NORWAY – NORVEGE**
Johan Grundt Tanums Bokhandel,
Karl Johansgate 41/43, OSLO 1. ☎ 02-332980

**PAKISTAN**
Mirza Book Agency, 65 Shahrah Quaid-E-Azam,
LAHORE 3. ☎ 66839

**PHILIPPINES**
R.M. Garcia Publishing House,
903 Quezon Blvd. Ext., QUEZON CITY,
P.O. Box 1860 – MANILA. ☎ 99.98.47

**PORTUGAL**
Livraria Portugal,
Rua do Carmo 70-74. LISBOA 2. ☎ 360582/3

**SPAIN – ESPAGNE**
Libreria Mundi Prensa
Castelló 37, MADRID-1. ☎ 275.46.55
Libreria Bastinos
Pelayo, 52, BARCELONA 1. ☎ 222.06.00

**SWEDEN – SUEDE**
Fritzes Kungl. Hovbokhandel,
Fredsgatan 2, 11152 STOCKHOLM 16.
☎ 08/23 89 00

**SWITZERLAND – SUISSE**
Librairie Payot, 6 rue Grenus, 1211 GENEVE 11.
☎ 022-31.89.50

**TAIWAN**
Books and Scientific Supplies Services, Ltd.
P.O.B. 83, TAIPEI.

**TURKEY – TURQUIE**
Librairie Hachette,
469 Istiklal Caddesi,
Beyoglu, ISTANBUL, ☎ 44.94.70
et 14 E Ziya Gökalp Caddesi
ANKARA. ☎ 12.10.80

**UNITED KINGDOM – ROYAUME-UNI**
H.M. Stationery Office, P.O.B. 569, LONDON SE1 9 NH, ☎ 01-928-6977, Ext. 410
or
49 High Holborn
LONDON WC1V 6HB (personal callers)
Branches at: EDINBURGH, BIRMINGHAM, BRISTOL, MANCHESTER, CARDIFF, BELFAST.

**UNITED STATES OF AMERICA**
OECD Publications Center, Suite 1207,
1750 Pennsylvania Ave, N.W.
WASHINGTON, D.C. 20006. ☎ (202)298-8755

**VENEZUELA**
Libreria del Este, Avda. F. Miranda 52,
Edificio Galipán, Aptdo. 60 337, CARACAS 106.
☎ 32 23 01/33 26 04/33 24 73

**YUGOSLAVIA – YOUGOSLAVIE**
Jugoslovenska Knjiga, Terazije 27, P.O.B. 36,
BEOGRAD. ☎ 621-992

Les commandes provenant de pays où l'OCDE n'a pas encore désigné de dépositaire peuvent être adressées à :
OCDE, Bureau des Publications, 2 rue André-Pascal, 75775 Paris CEDEX 16
Orders and inquiries from countries where sales agents have not yet been appointed may be sent to
OECD, Publications Office, 2 rue André-Pascal, 75775 Paris CEDEX 16

**OECD PUBLICATIONS, 2, rue André-Pascal, 75775 Paris Cedex 16 - No. 35.363 1975**

**PRINTED IN FRANCE**